61, HOW SOME WHEELS WENT ROUND.

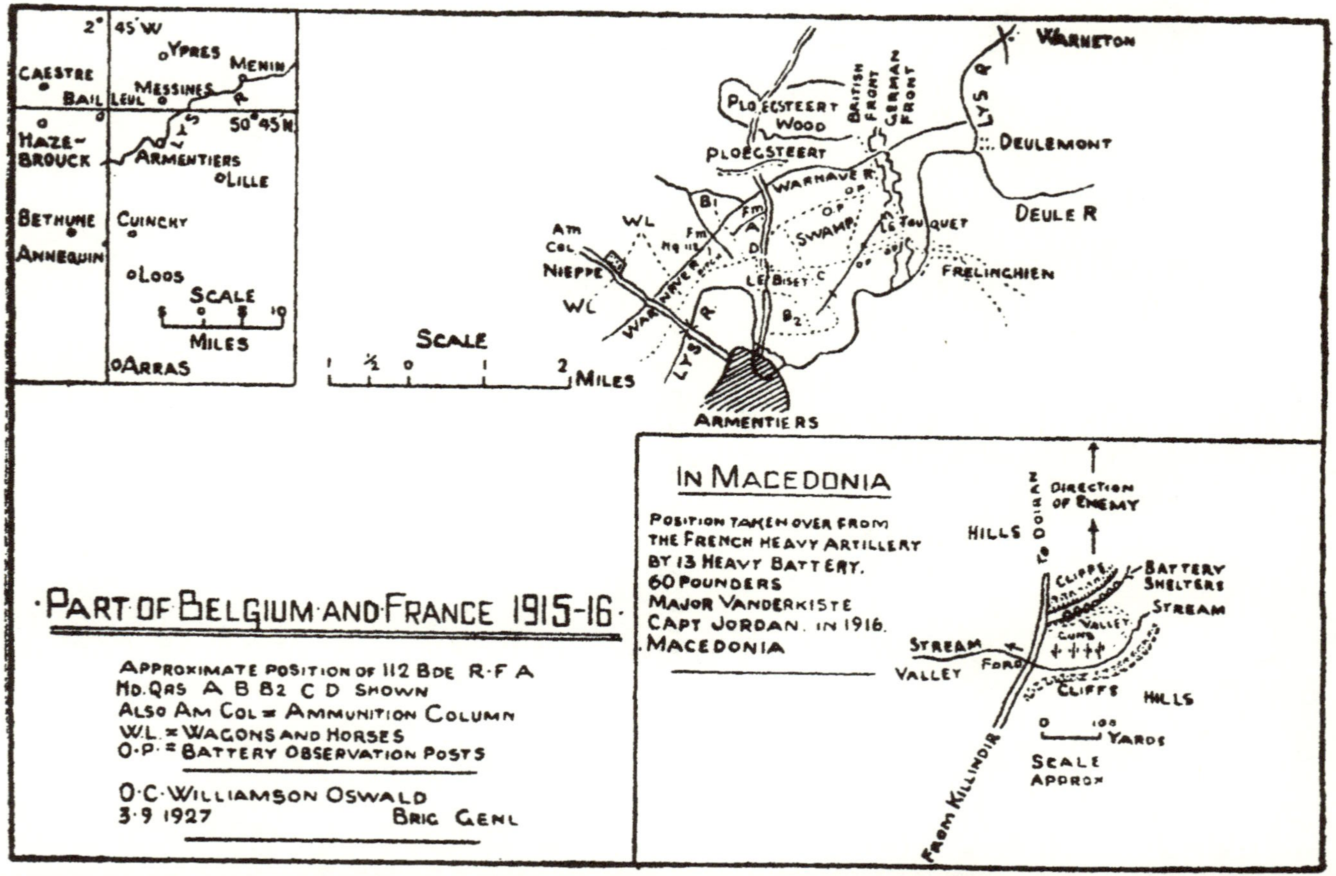

·PART OF BELGIUM AND FRANCE 1915-16·
APPROXIMATE POSITION OF 112 BDE R·F·A
HD.QRS A B B2 C D SHOWN
ALSO AM COL = AMMUNITION COLUMN
W.L. = WAGONS AND HORSES
O·P· = BATTERY OBSERVATION POSTS
O·C·WILLIAMSON OSWALD
3·9 1927
BRIG GENL
2° 45' W
YPRES
MENIN
CAESTRE
BAILLEUL
MESSINES
50° 45' N
HAZEBROUCK
ARMENTIERS
LILLE
BETHUNE
CUINCHY
ANNEQUIN
LOOS
SCALE
MILES
ARRAS
WARNETON
PLOEGSTEERT WOOD
BRITISH FRONT
GERMAN FRONT
LYS R
DEULEMONT
PLOEGSTEERT
WARNAVE R
DEULE R
SWAMP
LE TOUQUET
AM COL
NIEPPE
WL
FRELINGHIEN
LE BISET
SCALE
MILES
ARMENTIERS
IN MACEDONIA
POSITION TAKEN OVER FROM THE FRENCH HEAVY ARTILLERY BY 13 HEAVY BATTERY.
60 POUNDERS
MAJOR VANDERKISTE
CAPT JORDAN. IN 1916.
MACEDONIA
DIRECTION OF ENEMY
HILLS
TO DOIRAN
CLIFFS
BATTERY SHELTERS
STREAM
VALLEY
GUNS
FORD
CLIFFS
HILLS
YARDS
SCALE APPROX
FROM KILLINDIR

61,

HOW SOME WHEELS WENT ROUND

By

BRIG.-GENERAL O. C. WILLIAMSON OSWALD,

C.B., C.M.G., F.R.G.S.,

late R.A., also 3rd Class of the Order of the Nile and
Cavaliere Ufficiale of the Crown of Italy.

✻

The Naval & Military Press Ltd

❖

Reproduced by kind permission of the Central Library,
Royal Military Academy, Sandhurst

Published by

The Naval & Military Press Ltd

Unit 10 Ridgewood Industrial Park,
Uckfield, East Sussex,
TN22 5QE England
Tel: +44 (0) 1825 749494
Fax: +44 (0) 1825 765701
www.naval-military-press.com
www.military-genealogy.com
www.militarymaproom.com   .

*In reprinting in facsimile from the original, any imperfections are inevitably reproduced
and the quality may fall short of modern type and cartographic standards.*

CONTENTS

PREFACE.

Dedicated to wife and children.

This little work has been put together as a record of some years that are notable. The idea is to show that Britain was not altogether unprepared for facing her crisis in the way it actually came: though perhaps unprepared for "might have beens" that did not come. It deals with little things, but such little incidents multiplied made a great whole.

It is given the name of 61, as it deals much with that group, and it was begun when the writer was 61. It is written in the third person, as it originally began as an impersonal report, while this style has the authority of some ancient and other writings. Attention may also be drawn to the explanation of Technical Terms at the end of the Work.

Acknowledgement is thankfully given to the many friends who have helped with details at no small trouble to themselves.

O. C. W. O.

December, 1928.

CHAPTER I.

IN future years it may be asked: what manner of men were these, who to England's great good fortune came out of obscurity, made up, regimentally officered or commanded, and fought with their units, and so helped to destroy the German Power? They disappeared again into obscurity, leaving, at best, a few lines in "Who's Who" to record their work. Generally for the Army and here so far as Artillery is concerned, this work may be defined as the making of a number of effective artillery batteries and brigades from civilian volunteers; in the second case as the making of these units from volunteers who, under the Earl of Derby's Scheme, gave in their names as prepared to serve when called on. Most of the staff of the 61st Heavy Artillery Group were "Derby" men.

The Signaller Corporal was Etchells, the Master of Hull Workhouse.* The head clerk

---

*Poor Law Institution.

was a skilled shorthand typist, Hollins, from a
business house in Rotherham. The Adjutant,
W. Matthews, of Yeoman birth from Lancashire, who had served in the Field Artillery,
notably at Campbellpore, and fought on the
N.W. Frontier of India and in China (Walder-
see's Expedition). At 48 or 50 he got a commission in the R.G.A. and brought to bear his
talents as a battery office clerk on such matters
as rations, comforts and ammunition returns.
A story connects him with the miraculous
production at a tense moment of a hundred
rounds of 6-inch ammunition, weighing at least
five tons, that existed as a secret and authorized
reserve in a gully in the Balkans about 4000
yards south of Lake Dorian. He is now back
at his trade, which is that of master-carpenter.
If he is as much master of it as he was of an
adjutancy, he should do well. The Medical
Officer was Hoar. The son of a London Dental
Surgeon, he wandered about the world, ultimately administering an island of the Fiji
Group, where the World War caught him. He
was refused leave to volunteer for the war, but
in some way he managed to arrive as an
R.A.M.C. Captain and Medical Officer of
the Group. He was a rigid disciplinarian
and confessed to having early military
knowledge, having been a Territorial driver
in his teens and trained at Aldershot.
He had an instinct for the malingerer,
but was skilful and cautious, so there

were no complaints of really sick men
having been refused treatment by him or
returned to duty when they should have been
in hospital. He was invaluable in Macedonia
and Palestine, as with his tropical experience
both his diagnosis and his preventative measures were thorough. In Macedonia the heavy
artillery carried out some miles of canalisation
of stagnant mosquito-breeding pools near battery positions along the front from the Vardar
River to Sal Grek De Popovo, which was the
Group front, as well as in the back areas near
Kalinova, Vergetor, and Hirsova during the
spring and summer of 1917; some also during
the late autumn of 1916.   The mosquitos were
very virulent anopheles, and before the 61st
Group had been a week on the Macedonian
front one man, Bootiman, a miner, was attacked
and died.

   With the winter of 1916-17 malaria disappeared for the time and did not start again
in the group until April, 1917, when it took a
milder form, and there were no deaths at Group
headquarters.   During its time of prevalence
an anti-mosquito paste was issued to men out
on night work, especially those exposed at sun-
set and just after.   This order was found
difficult to enforce, as the paste was applied on
the neck, hands and face and was liable to come
off on the coat collar and sleeves.   It was also
an unpleasant ointment to have on the skin.
However, the order was carried out, thanks to

continual inspection, and certainly the fever victims were not so frequent.

The winter of 1916-17 in Macedonia was cold, showery, and wet. There were snow blizzards from the north which came on with suddenness, and then the whole area from 12th Corps headquarters at Janes to the front line was either under snow or about 12 inches of mud. The sickness was not severe and confined itself to colds and bronchitis, which in most cases were treated locally. This was possible owing to the tact and knowledge of his job of Captain Hoar and to our being stationary at the time. The comforts and pleasant life that the convalescent sick were able to lead in the large casualty clearing stations and in the base hospitals were not an unmixed blessing. Men of weaker natures deteriorated, and when back at duty they were noticed to be constantly for the sick parade; while men who had not tasted these joys seemed much freer from minor and imaginary ailments. So Captain Hoar's local treatment was, with his knowledge, a great asset: he knew how far it was safe to go. It is sad to relate that after the war he was much shaken with malaria and died when endeavouring to gain his livelihood in South Africa.

The Orderly officer was J. C. Brookhouse. He was a City of London solicitor of 36, a Liveryman of the Skinners' Company, and son of an important South London medical man. His knowledge of the world can be imagined. He believed in good food for officers and men, and this went far to keep the Group in health when stores could possibly be obtained. In that way both the shops of Salonika and subsequently Cairo, and the N.A.C.B., or Navy and Army Canteens Board organization, served the Group well. It was strange and archaic to hear their food, whiskey, wine and beer priced in drachma —10d, or in leptas—1d, in Greece; or in piastres —2½d, when the Group went to Egypt and Palestine. With his assistance and that of Capt. Matthews, the adjutant, the Group's bivouacs, dug-outs and billets rapidly put on a reality of comfort, the batteries were put in the way of obtaining the same, and all ranks profited. Lieutenant Brookhouse had started the war as a special constable; later he gained a commission. Had he pushed his claims he could probably have started much higher than a 2nd Lieutenant, as he was an old-time garrison artillery volunteer and had worn the old pork-pie forage cap with silver band in camp and at gun practice at Shoeburyness. However, he explained he was not up to date and preferred the lowlier position. Later on he became a battery Captain and at the Armistice an acting Major. His duties were Intelligence, and under the circumstances of service in Macedonia he was Counterbattery Staff Officer, as will be explained later.

Stephens, Warn, Toon and many others helped (see notes 1 and 12) to make the Group headquarters and contributed to its successful career. Stephens was by 1916 an old soldier, having volunteered early in 1914. He was by profession an artisan; he became telephonist, batman and soldier servant to Oswald in 1914 in 112th Brigade, R.F.A., and so remained till after the Armistice. He is back again at his work and doing well.

CHAPTER 2.

IT will be seen from the previous chapter that the officers of the 61st Heavy Artillery Group, though not military men in the narrow sense of regular officers, had, all of them, at some time paid attention to military matters, though at the crucial period they were hidden away in that uninstructed civilian mass which Germany despised and which, with this partially instructed leven and with some expert leadership, was to destroy her ambitions. As a reality the partial instruction in military matters had in even hundreds of thousands of cases gone far; as we know that, taking only the South African War 1899 to 1902, there were 450,000 recipients of the South African War Medals, including many non-regulars.

Similarly among the rank and file of the Group there were men of sufficiently high mental powers to be earning their living in various skilled trades and administering important portions of the country's daily life. In the Group, London, the Midlands, Yorkshire and Lancashire were represented.

These points bring us in natural sequence
to the Commanding Officer, and, at the risk of
a short biography, is put before you an example
of what schooling and military life had done
from the date of France's debacle in 1870 to the
World Conflict of 1914 to 1920 to create a class
of regimental commanding officers who in their
scores were able to sustain this position,
although handicapped by a personnel in which
neither officers nor rank and file had any up to
date military knowledge. This is true in the
vast majority of cases and where a few up-to-
date regulars were present, as for instance in
the case of the Regimental Sergeant-Major of
the 61st Heavy Artillery Group, these men were
in a position some ranks higher than that to
which they were accustomed in 1914. Another
handicap was that neither the regimental commanding officer nor any of his officers were
Staff College trained. Such officers as had
Staff College training were very early required
for Staff duties; and as the war went on, even
as early as 1916 no Staff College officer was permitted to take up A and Q duties (see the
explanation of technical terms at the end
page 201, etc.), while in minor formations such
as a Brigadier-General's command no regular
officer was allowed for any staff duties outside
the Brigade Major's own work.

In the 61st Heavy Group Royal Garrison
Artillery we find Lt.-Col. O. C. Williamson
Oswald assumed command when the Brigade

was formed. It is not claimed that he is a type, but still some personality has to be taken or else the student cannot get a grasp of the nature of the officer of that day, so *faute de mieux* his career is taken, that of an ordinary regimental officer not in 1914 distinguished by any rewards and not Staff College trained.

In August, 1914, Lt.-Col. Williamson Oswald was 51 years of age. He claimed that the Great War was at least the tenth time he had been mobilised. These mobilisations were, three curiously enough against Russia in 1885 and 1886; once for Burma, 1887; three times for Waziristan in 1894, 1897, 1900; once for the Chitral Relief Force in 1895; once for the South African War in 1901; once for Thibet in 1910; once for Persia in 1911. Some were abortive, but all gave experience.

To return to early years. Born of soldier forbears, who on both father's and mother's sides, as a matter of pride could also claim the Plantaganet blood of King Edward III. through his sons of Clarence and of Gaunt; he had clear recollections of the French tragedy of 1870. His first cousin, half a Frenchwoman, was a refugee with his parents; and the horrors of German War were the constant theme of family talk, including shooting of suspected "francstireurs" without trial and the chapter of misery all now so well known as the method of "Kultur" at War.

He went to St. Peter's School, York, in 1872,

when 8 years old with his brother Charnock.
He began Latin at 8 and Greek at 9 years old,
also French and Mathematics, and by 14 after
the loss of his father he was pronounced fit to
try in due course for Woolwich Academy. His
father's death in 1877 was also serious finan-
cially, as his mother, a genius and artist, was
left with five children and about £400 a year to
support them. Luckily school fees for day boys
were only* £16 a year. In 1880 Oswald had his
first attempt for Woolwich. He was a bad writer,
largely due to the crude custom of making
children write long impositions, but he could
swim, row and play Rugby football, a game he
kept up till he was 45. His mother had wisely
given her children much liberty, and in consequence he knew somewhat about horseracing and
"spotting the winner" at York and Doncaster
and was able to know enough to avoid a hot pool
game in a York Hotel while enjoying billiards
or pool with those of his own power. He failed
in the summer examination in mathematics.
He received during the examination a blue
envelope, the contents of which said he had
failed. The humour of the candidates called
this communication a blue pill.

He had a friend, Daniel, who, with Allenby,
now a Viscount, had that same term failed from
Wren's the crammer for the Indian Civil Service. These boys, with others, were consequently too old for Woolwich, but were arrang-
ing to work for Sandhurst for the Christmas

---

*Circa

Examination 1880. As Oswald's uncle, Major Charles Ingleby Harrison, Royal (late Bengal) Engineers, was at home on leave, a devoted brother to Oswald's mother, Oswald had the good fortune to have £80 guaranteed him for three months' tuition at a crammer's. He, with Daniel, Allenby, and others, joined a new establishment under a genius called Adams, a former master at Wren's. In the winter of 1880 he was successful for Woolwich, 29th out of 350 candidates, while of the others Daniel became a Colonel and Allenby the Victor of Jerusalem, their military careers lying far apart.

Woolwich Academy was hard work. In 1883, not being good enough for the Royal Engineers, he took a fair place in the Royal Artillery. Both at Woolwich and while a young officer Oswald kept out of trouble, largely thanks to the liberty he had enjoyed when at home. This made escapades in public-houses seem dull, while to some few other cadets from the boarding houses of large public schools these pranks seemed to be a temptation. Also, he was anxious to live at a minimum expense. He owed his fees at the Academy to the generous action of his Uncle Charlie. These came to £80 a year, as he was charged on the basis of being the son of a Colonel. The narrow means of at least one other of the 40 cadets of his term must have been worse than his mother's, as the special rate for the poorest cadet was given to another boy. His father, James Williamson

(formerly Oswald), by his services had gained
the right for a free Indian Cadetship, but wisely
the family did not use this until absolutely
necessary for Charnock, the second son, who
entered the Indian Infantry, fought in Burma,
and there died in 1892. The third son Noel,
alas! failed to gain a regular commission
through the militia, and after various adventures gained a Bengal Police appointment, lived
a lonely and isolated life in the Naga Hills until
about 1905, when he was promoted to Sadiya,
an important " Political " administrative post
which he held with distinction until 1911, when
he was murdered by Abors, after having added
much geographical knowledge, notably by his
death raising the veil which hid the passage of
the Sanpo River from Thibet to India. This
geographical riddle was solved by those who, in
1912, were sent as the Abor Expedition to
avenge Noel Williamson's death.

In February, 1883, then, Oswald became a
Lieutenant Royal Artillery. There was no
2nd Lieutenant's rank at the time. His pay
was 5s 7d. He had to dine in mess nightly,
paying 2s 6d whether he was present or not,
and for a glass of port to drink the Queen's
health. He, therefore, found it not easy to
take the very moderate shilling breakfast and
lunch and to keep solvent. So both during the
three months at Woolwich and three months at
Shoeburyness, where, with more advanced
riding than a cadet learnt, he was training in

gunnery and science, he had to curtail the pleasure of mess breakfasts and lunches. His soldier servant cooked him something from the canteen, and he eked out his hunger with bread, butter and tins of cocoa and milk, probably much to the benefit of his digestion.

The outfit of a young artillery officer was a problem. Some firms in Woolwich had pretty well a monopoly, though it is a question whether everything they supplied was exactly in conformation with the Dress Regulations. However, they were " it," but their charges were some pounds per cent. higher than London firms. Our young Lieutenant wanted these pounds badly; and so, with expert advice from old soldier friends and cousins, he put together a kit which was never found fault with, except the spurs to his jack boots. What a kit and a glory that 1883 uniform was:—Blue helmet, gold-laced tunic, blue and gold-lace stable jacket, blue frogged patrol (with false collar in gold lace when the stable jacket was not worn), mess jacket, mess waistcoat, both richly laced with gold; riding pantaloons were blue with red stripes, as also were the long trousers called overalls, which were worn with black leather half-boots, called Wellington boots, carrying steel spurs in the " boxes " built into the boot heels. For mess and full dress the overalls had gold stripes down the leg instead of red, and the Wellington boots were of patent black leather with brass spurs. The boots for

mounted parades were black, higher in front
than the back and nearly up to the knee, and
had spurs under the ankle bone like hunting
spurs.   The belts were marvellous, a relic
mostly of former armaments, but now purely
ornamental. A sword in a steel scabbard tied
to a waist belt with two straps, and dangling
between the two straps, on three straps of its
own, a sabretasche or glorified map case which
never held a map. Over the left shoulder and
close under the right armpit was a broad,
curved strap whose duty was to hold exactly
in the middle of the back a small oblong case
which could hold some cigarettes, but in reality
it was a relic of the days when ball-cartridge
was carried on a strap hanging from the left
shoulder.   These belts, in full dress, were of
rich gold lace; in other dress they were of
white patent leather which cracked easily. For
India an outfit of white cotton drill uniform
was wanted, a jacket, for parades and mess,
buttoning to the throat with four ball buttons,
nota bene ye who have bagged this button for
the exclusive use of the Royal Horse Artillery.
There were also white overalls for mess and
dismounted parades; khaki cotton drill uniform
had existed, but in 1883-1884 it, like the rank of
Brigadier General (see note 2), had ceased to
exist. The Army was taking a breather under
Staff Colonels. The light of rational service uniform was dim and kept alight in only a few units,
such as the Punjab Frontier Force battalions

and in some few far-seeing India units whose
Colonels, with James Williamson, had realised
that Drab to fight in is a much better colour
than Red, once the musket becomes a rifle; and
in those days remember fighting was done in a
soldier's best clothes.

Six months of very valuable teaching
ensued—horsemanship, gunnery, and military
law principally; there were also glimmerings
that the decision of the Ordnance Committee
that muzzle-loaders were more reliable than
breach-loaders was being shaken. A specimen
breach-loading field-gun was on view at Shoeburyness, and the course included very sound
and thorough teaching on the principles of
keeping the discharged gunpowder to do its job
and not to waste it; also the duties of the rifling
in the bore; the history of the projectile in the
air, and so on. What was not grasped in those
days was the reasons of variability in shooting.
Generally the layer of the gun got the united
curses of men and officers.   It certainly
improved laying, though equally certainly it was
quite unfair.   In 1884, at Lucknow, Oswald
went to practice with 9-pounder muzzle-loaders
for the field batteries. The targets were bulls-
eyes of about two feet diameter at a distance of
600 yards, and hits counted; the distant range
was 1200 yards, and there was a target in the
middle of a space about the size of a tennis
court, all of which space counted.   The men
who aimed were men who were best in a purely

literary examination, and one was allowed to be a Sergeant. Clerks, being more literary, naturally competed most, and those who aimed the best shots among them got the badges. The batteries in India had just received range-finders, and the Majors were groping for some method of shooting efficiently with shrapnel. Luckily, a British Officer, a German scholar, came along and translated for the British the experiences of Germany in their war with the French in 1870. Oswald found in the Mess Library in Agra, in 1885, the whole story of the German field batteries in the big battles of 1870. He devoured it. Then Prince Kraft's " Letters on Artillery " came along, translated by Walford: " The first duty of artillery is to hit; the second to hit; the third to hit." This was happening everywhere. The young artillery-men were roused and found a renaissance with leaders in Lord Roberts and General Nairne. The true methods by which artillery can hit began to be evolved; the " bracket," one shot over, one shot short, and so ultimately on to the enemy lines, and the care with which improved guns could really make their shrapnel burst where they wanted them. By the South African War, in 1900, the artillery were a useful adjunct, but if anything went wrong, the layer or aimer of the gun was still blamed. Then the garrison artillery invented a method by which a reasonably accurate shore gun could hit a ship automatically. This did not always come off:

no use to blame the layer in these cases. Then some genius thought of other things which affected the course of the shell, of barometer, thermometer, of the density of the air, and the temperature both of air and charge: winds were known about already, but the field artillery would have none of it, and did not benefit until 1915.   The wear of guns also was explained, and in the Great War was most material to accuracy when the wear was calculated.

However, this is a long distance from Oswald in 1883. He was ordered to India, and embarked in September, at the time Mr Gladstone was having one of the periodic worries about the Suez Canal.   So the four 4000-ton Troopships, then the pride of the trooping service Royal Navy, were ordered to avoid the Suez Canal, and directed to go to India round the Cape of Good Hope.   Oswald, as a junior officer, was on the lower deck with port-holes so close to the water that they were never opened out of port.   The heat was great, and ventilation was assisted by canvas windsails.   Some slept in hammocks; the lights were candles in swinging lamps.   However, all was very jolly in that part of the ship which was called Pandemonium.   No one was allowed to sleep on deck.   All had to turn out in smart uniform, including for dinner the smart gold-lace mess uniform of those days.

On arrival at Cape Town, as Oswald had a cousin married to Dr Versfelt of Stellenbosch,

an old Cape-Dutch family, he was allowed the
four days' period of the stop to go by rail to
see his relatives. He had a pleasant visit to a
large house, almost a farm, among avenues of
large trees. The doctor, a very loyal man and
a student of Edinburgh University, with his
wife and numerous children, were very
friendly. Oswald got a day's quail shooting,
done over pointer dogs. It was his first shoot,
and, though not any good as a shot, he enjoyed
it. It was only a short time since the Glad-
stonian surrender to the Dutch-Boers of the
Transvaal at Majuba, and some one of the
neighbours made a remark derogatory of the
British, rather sneering. This Versfelt promptly
quelled. Oswald rather felt the position, so he
was not sorry when, in due time, he was sent to
South Africa, in 1901, for the war there, and
found matters in a very different state from the
British point of view, and that he was taking
his small part in making them so.

CHAPTER 3.

INDIA IN THE EIGHTIES.

THE whole voyage of the Serapis troopship to India, in 1883, took 42 days to Bombay. Once in India, Oswald was among friends. He spent a short time at Meerut, where he found his uncle, Colonel Charles Ingleby Harrison, R.E. Here also was the 26th Punjab Infantry, his father's regiment, in which, in 1877, he had died.

Only a few hours had elapsed before the celebrated senior Indian Officer, Subedar Major Abdulla Khan, possessor of many Indian Orders and the Indian Order of Merit for bravery, came over to see him. He embraced Oswald as the baby first-born son of his beloved Colonel: a baby whom he had carried in his arms years before. He spoke much of the Colonel and leader who had commanded the 26th from 1857 to 1877, from Lieutenant to full Colonel.

Later on at the Delhi Manœuvres of 1885, D Battery 4th Brigade R.A., in which Oswald served, was in the same division as the 26th Punjab Infantry. One day the battery officers' camp was visited by an array of the whole of the Indian Officers of the 26th Punjab Infantry,

headed by Abdulla Khan, in all their decorations
and medals. A great honour indeed. All were
presented by the Subedar Major, and all presented the hilts of their swords for the boy to
touch, a great honour, as Kipling puts it, only
vouchsafed to children and Viceroys. A very
proud moment. Many had known Oswald as a
child. One Sikh warrior he distinctly remem-
bers, with a white flowing beard, not curled up
and tied behind his ears as is the present Sikh
fashion, but flowing as is depicted in pictures
of British battles in the wars of the 1840's
against the Sikhs under Ranjit Singh.

From 1883 to 1887 Oswald served in D
Battery 4th Brigade, now 18th R.F.A., at Lucknow and Agra. This was a battery with
Peninsular traditions. Major Lawrie, Captain
Kuper, and Lt. Beatson were the other officers,
and much good sport, including the driving of
a four-in-hand, pig-sticking, polo, and duck and
snipe shooting were enjoyed. The guns, alas!
were still 9-pounders. The only available pony
Oswald had for pig-sticking was a 12½ hands
chestnut, very strong and well bred, but which
gave him more tosses than pig-sticking. It
cost seventy-five rupees—say, £4 10s—and was
well worth it. Later, when owing to mobilisa-
tion, an artillery subaltern was allowed two
chargers, Oswald used one of these, and got
nine first spears in the hot weather of 1886 at
Agra. The money tightness at that time is
exemplified by the fact that Oswald could not

afford to share the lunches taken out by the
Club, nor to pay an entrance fee of 32 rupees,
less than two pounds, for his two chargers for
the Multra pig-sticking cup, though his chances
were as good as most, and he knew much of the
ground ridden over.   His experience of pig-
sticking is that one severe fall for horse and
rider must be expected every day one rides to
pig, and that a horse is stauncher if he is not
ridden exactly in the footsteps of the boar but
a bit on the near side.   One method of aug-
menting his pay of 225 rupees a month, plus
30 rupees a month allowance for charger and
saddlery, including buying the charger, was to
get the extra billet of the acting adjutancy at
Agra.   This acting job was given him by Lt.-
Col. Pitt, R.A., a delightful commanding officer,
commanding all the artillery at Agra.   He
learnt there office routine, while as Mess
secretary he learnt accounts.   In those days
promotion examinations could be taken any
time, as all were Lieutenants, there being no
rank junior to that.   Oswald accordingly got
through his promotion examination for Captain
on practically his recollections of what he had
learnt at the Royal Military Academy, called
the "Shop" in military slang.   Later, regulations came out to prevent such early passing of
promotion examinations, and the examination
was made a much greater business, but this did
not affect Oswald.
    In the 1886 hot weather many went on leave

from Agra. Oswald tested a thermometer by placing it on a clipped hedge, face up, and got a temperature of 180 degrees Fahrenheit from the direct sun's rays. The going on leave of Captain C. P. Triscott, R.A., the Ordnance Officer of Agra Fort, led to an offer to Oswald to act in Triscott's place for three months. This meant a very hot drive to the Fort, about two miles away, behind the small chestnut pony; then office work for an indefinite number of hours, and also the company of Hon. Captain Fraser, a subordinate of the Ordnance Department, who had been previously in the Horse Artillery. Oswald never saw him in uniform, but he must have possessed the Indian Mutiny Medal of 1857. He had many stories. He was Sergeant Major, he said, of a troop or battery of Bengal Horse Artillery when commanded by Olpherts, V.C., called Hell-fire Jack. The farrier wore a scarlet coat, and so, in action, was much shot at. The horses were all stud-bred chestnut stallions. They had syces. Some horses required two syces or grooms. The gunners were British long-service men enlisted by the East India Company. The Detachment of six gunners rode the six gun horses, and there was a sergeant in command. The seats on the gun limber were occupied by Indian gun lascars, generally high-caste men, who, in action, held the gun team after the gunners had dismounted, the team being drawn up in rear of the gun in action. The two limber gunners appear to have ridden the two pole horses, as there was pole draught.   One limber gunner was in the unpleasant position of having a "pussy-foot" horse, who, ere he let the gunner mount, would smell him over, and if he smelt spirits no force could make him stand still for the "mount," while with his teeth he tried to tear off the saddle of the horse in front.   Capt. Fraser said the battery was part of the British White Force in Mian Mir Lahore, when the Indian Mutiny was beginning.   The General at Lahore paraded the troops, and in the course of manœuvre he got the Bengal infantry battalions into close order, company behind company, and faced and flanked by the small British force, with the horse artillery in action directly in front of the Bengal battalions.   It was a pre-arranged piece of manœuvre only known to the white officers and the white rank and file.   The white infantry were loaded with ball and the guns with grape.   The Bengal Infantry had no ammunition on parade.   The General ordered the Bengal Infantry to lay down their arms, as though they were as yet loyal, and he hoped would continue loyal, it was not safe for them to keep their arms owing to influences that might move them later.   He said ten would be counted, and if they had not grounded arms by then they would be fired on. The counting began; about the middle of it the General called out in English to the white officers of the Bengal battalions: "Gentlemen, at the word 'fire!' try and save yourselves by falling on your faces, but remember you die for your country." The counting was nearly over when a sort of muttering began in the Bengal Infantry ranks, and then with a crash the arms were thrown down. "Right about face," roared the officers of the Bengal regiments. "Quick March." Away they went. "Front limber up," and the horse artillery advanced without more ado straight over the derelict muskets of the Bengal battalions and came into action the other side. So ended this historical incident.

1885 was the year of trouble with Russia over the Afghan Frontier where Persia and Russia approach it. Oswald was ordered up to join, temporarily, P battery 1st Brigade at Rawalpindi, where a large troop concentration was taking place. Lord Dufferin, Sir F. Roberts, the Amir of Afghanistan, and many celebrities were present. The battery was, with other field batteries, in camp on Khanna plain. The mud was so bad that the review was arranged to be only a defile past the Amir and his bodyguard of assembled Usbegs and Afghans at Rawalpindi fort, so as to save the troops from marching in the mud of the Khanna plain, and only to move the troops along the hard roads. The defilade was a very impressive one, until the Amir expressed his opinion that he had seen some of the troops now before him in a previous appearance at the

commencement of the defilade. So, after all,
the troops had to be turned out again on the
open plain, and this convinced the Amir it was
no stage-army business.   One very interesting
visitor came to see the field batteries, Colonel
Michael Biddulpp, R.A.   He pointed to the row
of field batteries, all alas! 9-pounder muzzle-
loaders, with brass studs or lumps on their
shells for purposes of rifling, which could only
give a very poor show over about 2000 yards'
range, and whose shrapnel were timed to burst
with a clumsy wooden-fuze arrangement.   He
remarked, "I have up there three batteries
which could take on and knock out all you nine
or more batteries."   He referred to the British
Mountain Artillery, then armed with the original
7-pounder screw-gun, a weapon much superior
in shooting powers to the 9-pounder.   It was,
indeed, a muzzle-loader, but it had an accurate
metal time fuze to burst the shrapnel, and the
shell was more scientifically fitted to the rifling
inside the gun, having a saucer-shaped copper
plate or gas check on its base.   This plate
enclosed the gun-powder gas behind the shell,
giving it much more accuracy than the brass-
studded shell of the 9-pounder, which allowed
much of the gun-powder gas to rush past the
shell.   Indeed, so satisfactory did the higher
powers, led by General Adye, R.A., consider
these gas checks that it took Britain years
before a breach-loader was permitted either in
the artillery or the Navy. Luckily, the struggle

c

with Russia did not come off in the days of such backward armament as the 9-pounder guns and muzzle-loading Naval big guns.

It is extraordinary how, with the finest fighting qualities in their men, the British men in power are continually scamping their weapons. Luckily, the Great War of 1914 found us with the 18-pounder field gun, which was completely up-to-date, except, perhaps, for its time fuze; but even then the heavy artillery had to be content with the 60-pounder gun, and that in small quantities. Only one giant howitzer existed, luckily it (the 9.2-inch) did exist, so that others could be made from its pattern. The smaller howitzer, the old pattern 6-inch, could have gone out with the Expeditionary Force in 1914, but were only called up for the battles of the Aisne. The same thing happened in the South African War before Lord Roberts took over command. India had offered 40-pounder heavy siege guns, but these were refused, and the Navy had to improvise an armament of heavy guns to take on the Boers in 1899. The reason is not far to seek. It is very natural that at peace manœuvres the spectacular should get undue value, and that the heavy artillery, firing imaginary shells and blank cartridges from some far-away position, should not get credit for the devastation it would create. Consequently, when war comes, the absolute necessity for heavy guns has a way of getting forgotten. They are so cumbrous and require so much transport that it is easier to leave them out of a plan, than to worry out some way of getting them along. Lord Roberts made no such mistake in South Africa when, after Buller's defeat at Colenso, he took over command, but had and used his heavy guns, with which Oswald served in 1901, having a battery of 5-inch guns firing up to a range of 6½ miles.

As regards mountain guns, it was somewhat due to Oswald's four years' intermittent service on the Artillery Committee, namely, from 1909 to 1912, as related in Chapter 8, that the shielded gun, the 2.75-inch, was in existence in 1914 for the mountain gunners, and that the 20-pounder howitzer was kept alive as a potential weapon and not discarded as being impracticable. The 20-pounder howitzer called the 3.7-inch, is at the date of writing quite the longest ranging and most powerful pack howitzer in the world; it fought in the Great War in 1917 and later, and was highly satisfactory.

CHAPTER 4.

AN INDIAN BATTERY.

PROVIDENCE was merciful in bringing no Russian War in 1885 or 1886. The British responsibilities luckily turned to work more suited to advance the British Power and its talent for the upsetting of cruelty. Burma under Thebaw was a shambles. This touched Oswald, as more Indian mountain batteries were to be raised. Oswald in 1886, after three years' hard work, had just passed the Hindustani language test, called the Higher Standard, which opens most Indian billets to those who pass it. Captain C. P. Triscott, R.A., got an offer to leave the Indian Ordnance Department and raise No. 1 Bengal Mountain Battery. He offered a subaltern's appointment in it to Oswald, whose name had already been entered for Indian Artillery. The pay was good, being 150 rupees—say—£9 a month, better than that of a field or garrison battery. This began a new chapter in Oswald's life.

A small number of men selected from the Sikhs and Punjabi Mohammedans of the Indian Mountain Batteries of the Punjab Frontier Force formed the nucleus. They were sent out to enlist and, furthermore, to train the new recruits. Oswald joined at Rawalpindi, and found every hour of the day occupied in training work. It was realised that the battery and its sister, called Nos. 1 and 2 Bengal Moutain Batteries, were required for the much-needed relief of No. 4 Hazara and No. 1 Bombay Mountain Batteries in Burma. So Oswald and his brother subalterns, Bruce Lane and Pasley, with, for a short time, Drake (lent while Lane was sick), had a further incentive to get No. 1 Bengal Mountain Battery ready. This went on all the winter of 1886-87. The Duke of Connaught was the General at Rawalpindi, and used often to ride to the battery lines to see its progress. He was very friendly and helpful.

Oswald went in March, 1887, with his battery to Burma. They were camped in Calcutta on the great level plain outside Fort William. In those days no one knew that malaria was carried by mosquito-bite, and mosquito nets were considered rather an effeminacy. So the troops suffered, but luckily on this occasion no malaria visited them. Here in Calcutta Captain Triscott met many friends; General Chesney, R.E., the celebrated Indian statesman and Military Member, and Mr Hensman, Editor of the Pioneer Newspaper, both were guests at a farewell battery dinner. Hensman later in Simla became a good friend of Oswald's when Hensman was Rudyard Kipling's boss. Kipling was writing (this in 1889)

the "From Sea to Sea" letters, and Hensman
tried to edit some of their exuberance, so he told
Oswald.   For   years   Hensman   guided   the
Pioneer.   In 1909 he and Oswald discussed the
Liberal budget and super-tax, which to them,
who were poor, did not appear an unreasonable
tax for rich people.   In 1914 Hensman was in
England and sent the Pioneer Newspaper in
India very early news of the first battle of the
Marne, the battle of the Aisne in September,
1914, and of the British confrontation of the
Germans at Ypres, which, he wired, gave the
Germans the surprise of their lives and which
saved the Channel Ports.   All these messages
greatly heartened the people in India and confirmed their loyalty to Britain.

General Chesney had been in France in the
War in 1870.   He was a great authority on military affairs, and as a young officer about 1872
he had written "The Battle of Dorking," which
gave a startling account of an invasion of
England, as it appeared possible to thinking
soldiers of that day.   It was one of the calls to
arms made most courageously but opposed by
the old timers, headed by the Horse Guards
Staff and Parliament.   However, the chorus
grew; Garnet Wolseley added his voice, crying
that the British were sacrificing the essentials
of modern war to red coats and to theatrical
spectacles.   Wolseley made Oswald and others
reflect by writing the soldiers' pocket-book,
taken again largely from the old Artillery book

of the same nature. Wolseley even went so far
as to say that a General officer in a scarlet tunic
and hat with white cock's feathers in it was
uselessly dressed, reminded him of an Italian
organ-grinder's monkey with its comic travesty
of the same uniform, and was about as practical
from a military point of view. Well, Wolseley
and also Triscott's friend, General Chesney, in
1887 had begun to see their reward in reform
of the Army in India at least.   Lord Roberts
had been made Commander-in-Chief in India:
he had begun to make order out of the chaotic
arrangements of 1885 and 1886, when India was
endeavouring to mobilise against Russia; serviceable uniforms of khaki of a sensible and
comfortable nature had been introduced, and
the Army in India was rapidly becoming a fighting machine. This meeting with General
Chesney was most interesting to both Oswald
and his uncle, Charles Harrison, who was at the
time also a guest at this dinner, he being at the
time Chief Engineer for irrigation to the
Government of Bengal. Chesney and the two
relatives talked together; Oswald asked about
his 1870 Franco-German War experiences.
Chesney said that after the disaster of Sedan
there was little that a soldier could learn, as
once Sedan was over the German movements
were not seriously opposed: " It was like cutting
butter with a hot knife."

Burma eventuated for Oswald after Calcutta; the troops were railed to some spot on

the Irrawaddy and then by flat-bottomed river steam via Thayetmyo, the frontier of Lower Burma, up country. Oswald's brother Charnock, a war-worn veteran by now, met him at one of the halts; he was now with the 16th Bengal Infantry, keeping order in a large district.

The Burma affair is worthy of relation at some further time. Oswald's experiences were much those of Kipling's heroes, though, of course, in a minor and not so romantic manner. There was hard jungle fighting and heavy losses and much malarial fever. At present, however, organization to which success in fighting is largely due must be taken up and related. Ultimately, of course, it is the individual courage and obstinacy of the individual fighting man which give victory, and more, which delay defeat and prevent disaster, but to gain decisive victory this individual must be fully armed and **organized.**

CHAPTER 5.

WITH Oswald's transfer, in 1886, from D Battery 4th Brigade R.A., a field battery, to the Indian Mountain Artillery a series of new experiences commenced which were to culminate in the intensive training of large masses of artillerymen in the Great War.

As related in Chapter 4, Oswald joined Captain (the late Brigadier-General) C. P. Triscott's No. 1 Bengal Mountain Battery at Rawalpindi. The Duke of Connaught was in command there and took an interest in the effort. The object was to raise two batteries; the second one was under Smith, senior subaltern Fuller (now a Brigadier-General), at Lahore. These two batteries were wanted as quickly as possible to proceed to Upper Burma, which was in process of being conquered. Thebaw, the King of Burma, had been too cruel and impossible to deal with, even for British politicians; and the great Lord Dufferin took Burma, with Lord Roberts as Commander-in-Chief and Sir George White as Commander in

Burma.   The work was mostly guerilla warfare; small columns of infantry, artillery, and mounted men.   The mounted men were really mounted riflemen, as there was no charging with sword or lance to be done, and so the training was the inception of that required later on for South Africa, where M.I. (Mounted Infantry) columns were the ultimate main arm.

On looking back, it is strange to observe how the preparation for war methodically evolves from previous wars.   Burma produced the Mounted Infantry which wiped up matters in South Africa.   South Africa, in 1880 and in 1899, brought realization of the cost of frontal attacks.   It produced the rifleman, the accurate shot, the necessity for the uniform-sized divisional formation in all parts of the empire, the thinking in units of divisions instead of in battalions and batteries, the use of barbed wire, the use of khaki and concealment of troops in civilised war; the use of long-ranged guns, helio-signalling and a general staff.   The Russo-Japanese War confirmed this, added the use of telephones, close support of Infantry by pack Artillery and machine guns.   Much was ignored, but enough was remembered and noted to make our share of the war in 1914 creditable to our training, and we emerged in 1919 with the lessons learnt; of using really heavy long-range mobile guns, of scouting and bombing with aeroplanes, and also that the infantrymen was still the preponderant arm, but wanted to be armoured, or to be tank-assisted; that gas was a lethal weapon; that all warfare, if the sides are staunch and fairly equal, still comes to a time of trench-fighting. Also we learned that old-time warfare, open fighting, cavalry, real cavalry, not mounted infantry, mobility, horse artillery, were still useful where, as, for example, in the Near East a flank could be found, and there existed " a way round," even as at Colenso. The quotation mark means that these words were uttered to Sir Redvers Buller by the U.S.A. Attaché, after the British frontal attack at Colenso, in 1900, had failed with heavy loss: " Say, mister, is there no way round?" The curiosity of this battle of Colenso was the very beautiful " Operation Order " produced by General Clery, which would have got full marks in any examination—unfortunately, the northern bend of the Tugela River, which was the key of the position, seems to have been missed or ignored, with the result that the main attack had no chance of success, as it was dominated from the East, while no " way round " was found. The Infantryman, as usual, thought in hundreds of yards, when weapons were acting in thousands of yards. This seems a fault our Infantry always have and will have. It is not clear that even the 1914 war has cured them of it. It leads to much gallantry, but goodness, what losses! when sudden bursts of long-range rifles and guns come into play. On the other hand, the staff,

if composed of comparatively young cavalry-
men, as often happens, think in distances of the
horse, so that when Infantry have to move they
find themselves called upon to move some
impossible distance, instead of the ten or twelve
miles, which is all that any careful General
should expect to get out of his Infantry in a
day: this happened to the 21st and 24th
Divisions in 1915 at the Battle of Loos.

All this has taken us a long way from
raising a battery. First, in Rawalpindi, Triscott was very busy with recruiting and
equipment. The training was left to the
Subalterns, Pasley, Bruce Lane and Williamson
(Oswald). It was grasped that intensive training of the new recruits was necessary, in order
to produce a mountain battery fit for fighting
in Burmese jungles, and to do so within the next
four or five months, when, with the Spring, the
Indian Mountain Batteries fighting in Burma
would require relief or reinforcements.
Intensive training necessitated, of course, a
preliminary catching of suitable recruits. In
those days—and, indeed, practically still—the
best recruiters are men of the battery in which
the recruit has to serve. The result is that,
with a nucleus of Indian Officers and good men
promoted into the new battery, not only have
classes of instruction for the recruits to be
formed, but also some of the best-type men of
good fighting families have to be sent off as
recruiters. Both in 1886 and again in 1907,

when Oswald raised 32 Indian Mountain Battery, now 12 Poonch (not Punch please) Mountain Battery, it was needful to send out recruiters. During this recruiting, large batches were successfully brought in to points on the Punjab Railways, to which a British Officer, generally the Commander of the battery, made a hasty journey. He saw and verified the suitability of the men and got them railed down to the nearest medical officer; after which the passed men were sworn into the army as recruits; their final swearing-in and acceptance depended upon their progress as recruits; and the batch then joined their battery for training. It was wisest to give all credit for the batch to the Indian recruiting centres concerned; this made for smooth working; much as in 1921 and 1923 Oswald gave credit to the local Labour Exchanges, when jobs for unemployed ex-Artillerymen in London had been found. Great is the power of statistics and great is the lubricating virtue of tact. Further, in India, it was wise for the British Officer to stand by his recruits until they were in the train for the Battery. Every recruit had the power to withdraw his service until he came in as a recruit after his medical examination. Many intrigues went on in those days from rival parties of recruiters, and really good recruits sometimes developed unaccountable reluctance at the last moment, which the presence of their Sahib, the British Officer, was generally able to dispel. This tie between the recruit and the British Officer who brought him into the army is, in India, a very real one, and long may it be possible to give the soldier's soul a chance and allow enlistment to be a voluntary act. Years after, in 1919, when Oswald was the General at Ismailia on the Suez Canal, during the Pan-Islam movement and the rebellion in Egypt, 32 Indian Mountain Battery and also 29 Indian Mountain Battery were there, as well as an offspring, 38 Indian Mountain Battery; these three batteries commanded by Phillips, Somerville, and Lindsay respectively. There were great re-unions, and Oswald made a point of shaking hands with his old friends of all batteries, while he was often accosted by one who would say, "I am one of your recruits, sahib." So is love and good feeling preserved.

The recruiting in the case of the Kitchener Armies (called officially the New Armies) in the Great War, in 1914-15 and '16, was also by voluntary enlistment. To Oswald voluntary enlistment means an intense conviction that the man or woman, in spite of all dangers, spiritual and bodily, finds in his or her soul a call to a very trying duty—the serving of the country in a manner that is never easy or convenient. In this is included the voluntary enlistment of the old regular army, territorials and the new regular army commenced in 1919. The few cases of " down and outers " does not affect the

matter in his mind, and even in their case it is
a call to a nobler life.

Oswald, in 1914, was serving in an Indian
Mountain Brigade as Lt.-Colonel in Abbottabad.
After the first excitement of the declaration of
war and the relief in honest people's minds that
Britain was going to raise trouble about the
desecration of neutral little Belgium, it was
found that the Indian Army and the country
acted as was expected, and were all out to aid
the " Raj."—the Empire.   There were some
cold feet high up in the Government, but no
matter.

Alethea was a baby and Praxeda and
Ingleby were children.   In October, 1914,
Oswald's two batteries disappeared* on missions
in seperate directions; and Luke, the Artillery
Headquarter-man, wrote soothing messages to
Oswald, then in command for a few days of the
Abbottabad Brigade, of which Capt. Loveday,
R.G.A., was Brigade-Major.   These soothing
messages materialised into an order for Oswald,
with his wife and family, to go to England.
Oswald was to report for duty at the War
Office.

Everything that could be was sold, except
saddles and war-like gear.   The Ford car,
" two years old, but little used," went for £80
to a Frontier Police Officer, through the good
offices of Subedar Badiulzaman, 46th Punjabs,
an Afridi and a grandson of that great Abdulla,
26th Punjabs, the friend of Colonel James

*See Note 23.

Williamson (formerly Oswald) Oswald's father.

The move was a trying one, but the mother, Meta Williamson Oswald, had all matters efficiently in hand as usual, and what with sterilised milk for the babe and care for the two elder ones, England and London were reached safely in health about December 8th, 1914, by the P. and O. steamer, *Egypt*. Stewards and stewardesses on board did their duty well, although the passengers were largely wives and children of soldier-officers, whose purses were perhaps not available for such tips as first-class P. and O. stewards generally expect. The weather down to Bombay was cool, and the Wessex Division of Territorials passed the train, they were proceeding up into India to replace Regulars, both British and Indian, going to various theatres. They were singing "Tipperary." This patriotic division may have felt sore at not going to France, but before it was over the long war gave them every chance of battle and danger. A streak of good news arrived for Oswald's party as they went south to Bombay. In November, 1914, the "Emden," a German cruiser, had been sunk in the Indian Ocean, near Cocos Islands, by the Australian cruiser, "Sydney." There was great rejoicing, as her career of destruction had included Madras, the Malay States, and many merchant steamers in Indian waters. The Captain, Müller, was no "Hun," for he saved lives though he sank ships. Now-a-days, this is not

expected, and in the next war it is supposed
every one will be counted a fighter either on
land and sea, even babes; a curious commentary
on civilisation's progress.   The P. and O.
Egypt carried lights, and lighted cabins in
the seas south of Egypt and in the Mediterranean.   Passing through the Suez Canal at
the end of November there was war; the Turks
had been moving, and troops from India, with
Lancashire Territorials, were in charge here;
while Egypt was simmering down after the
making of the Protectorate of Egypt, with the
brand-new title of Sultan given to the new
Khedive Fuad.   Hilmi, having taken the side of
the Turks, was deposed.

Malta was called at and also Gibraltar,
where many captured German merchant ships
were lying interned, as well as the gallant
armed auxiliary cruiser, *Carmania*, a liner
which lately had sunk her enemy, *Cap
Trafalgar*, in the South Atlantic.   The rigours
of war began in the Atlantic, through which the
Egypt sailed without lights, mysterious
stoppages were made, possibly to signal to
men-of-war.   It was very rough in the English
Channel, and, as by the rules, the British ports
were closed by night, a terrible night was spent
lying off England.   Meta Oswald and the other
women showed good nerve, but the anxiety of
cruising and waiting for the " doors to open "
all that rough night, with submarine dangers
close by, was a great test of nerve.   Near here

D

H.M.S. *Formidable* was torpedoed about a couple of months later, while the whole English Channel was alive with alarms during those dark and stormy nights.

London was reached, and orders were given after a week's wait. Oswald was sent to raise a Field Artillery Brigade at Frome. He was asked if he would do so by Lt.-Colonel Arthur Young, although Oswald was a garrison gunner. It seemed no time for making difficulties. The eighteen months spent with the 112th R.F.A. Brigade was a very happy time, and officers and men rejoiced in their work. On leaving the Brigade in March, 1916, Oswald felt a great wrench of parting. Afterwards, friends of hers in 112 sent a gift to Meta Williamson Oswald, a large, indeed a colossal, silver tea-tray and service, as a parting gift to her who had helped so much during the times in Frome, Heytesbury, Winchester, and Aldershot to keep touch and friendliness amongst them all. Oswald might have done better for himself had December, 1914, to March, 1916, been spent with his own branch, the Royal Garrison Artillery. But to take up the work immediately offered was the patriotic thing to do; and that his name, with other R.G.A. Colonels with R.F.A. brigades, did not come out as Brigadier-Generals R.G.A., when the great R.G.A. re-organization was made in February, 1916, is a matter that seems immaterial. All's well that ends well, and blessed are they who expect nothing, but it does seem wrong that of those early 1916 R.G.A. Brigadiers, none reached the honour of Knighthood, although Buckle and Tancred each served as Major-General Royal Artillery.

The 112th R.F.A. Brigade was part of the divisional artillery of the 25th Division. No one can do better than read Gilbert Frankau's book, " Peter Jackson, Cigar Merchant," to get a thoroughly good idea of the experiences Oswald's Brigade went through in training. Frankau's 24th Division actually belonged to the same group of divisions of Kitchener's Army, namely, the 21st to 26th Divisions of the New Army. For the 25th Division R.F.A., Frome remained for the winter of 1914-15 a refuge and training-centre. The men were lodged under cover—some in large factories, some in billets, and some in tents. It would have been possible to billet them all, but in that case the training would have suffered, and it was obvious that the spirit of all these volunteers and patriots was absolutely against comfort at the cost of delay. Delay in getting on with the war was the thing which made the men restless. Collected together by voluntary enlistment, after having sacrificed their comforts, their beds and houses, their wages and trades, after having said good-bye to wife or dear ones, these men, mostly from the north of England and the Midlands, talking the language Oswald associated with his youth in Yorkshire;

all wanted to get on with their training at all
costs and to get fighting with a view of being
through with it and back home again. If anything extra had been needed to rouse their
ardour, it was the attack of the German battle
cruisers against Hartlepool. As one man, who
enlisted as an artillery driver from Hartlepool,
said: "The streets were like butchers' shops!"
In his indignation he and thousands, perhaps
even a million, of Yorkshiremen and men of
Durham and Northumberland were induced to
enlist, many of them selecting the artillery,
simply because it was artillery that had
massacred Hartlepool.

CHAPTER 6.

TRAINING.

IN the training of men as field gunners and drivers for the war of 1914, Oswald's experience in No. 1 Bengal Mountain Battery in 1886, and in No. 32 Indian Mounted Battery in 1907, came in very usefully. In the former case, viz., 1886, the calls to be ready for Burma were very insistent. All cases may, therefore, be taken together. Intensive training is required when active service in the immediate future is expected. By intensive training for artillery is meant, roughly, the process of teaching only so much of the team work required in a batery as will permit the whole work of the battery to carry on; first, under favourable circumstances and with the more knowledgable ones in the battery prompting the rest; and later with all knowing their particular duties very well and knowing the rest of the team work partially. Such, then, was the line taken by the light of experience in 1886, 1908, and in 1914.

The officers and drivers were taught to ride. Early in 1915 a rumour rose that horses were available, but no saddlery, no bits, no gear at

all. Oswald said, "Send them along," the
invaluable adjutant Parkins, late a pay sergeant
R.F.A., and the Battery Commanders, Norton,
a R.F.A. Regular, back from France; a staunch
Scot with his wife, Fraser; D. Campbell, an old
R.G.A. Mountain Gunner, who later received
the Military Cross, and was killed in 1917 near
Messines; A. Barker from the ranks of King
Edward's Horse, a man of fiery energy, now a
D.S.O. and somewhere in China; ably helped by
Harold Vincent, now in the oilfields and a
successful engineer, whose wife and daughter
so often share his adventures and experiences.
They were assisted by the younger men, then
mostly 2nd Lieutenants R.F.A., of whom the
survivors are war-worn veterans, and Captains
and Majors with decorations, and many back in
civil life; Letts, Mackay, Christie Millar, P. Fry,
D. Carr (afterwards M.C.), Heron, Nowell-
Usticke, Hanson, Moore, and others.

Afterwards Capt. Auret joined B Battery,
fresh from fighting in German West Africa.
He was killed in France, a barrister and a keen
and conscientious gunner.

These in 112, and others in 110, 111 and 113
Brigades R.F.A., boldly undertook to receive as
many horses as could be sent, knowing that beyond a rope and webbing halter there were no
sort of horse trappings with them. Even the
rope and webbing halter had to go back to the
Remount department as soon as some other
fastening device was arranged for the horses;

and for weeks riding was taught on bare-back horses with rope halters for reins.

No matter; Oswald had vivid remembrances of mobs of mules sent up from Calcutta with F. E. Spencer, now D.S.O. and a Major, to Dehra Dun in 1907 in charge of inexperienced drivers, and then picketed in the open. All had gone well in 1907, so why not in 1915, especially with Frome opening her arms and her stables, so that all the horses had a shelter and a home ready, though alas! no gear? Frome did even better; it opened its shops; some saddles and much gear were found; ere long horse brushes instead of straw whisps appeared; some saddles were now supplemented by enough harness for about four gun teams. This was an adventure of Oswald's and Adjutant Parkins. The latter suggested " Moses " of London, the pre-war purchaser of worn-out artillery harness and other gear, as a likely place to find harness sufficiently serviceable to teach the recruits. So off Capt. Parkins went with Oswald's private cheque and returned with about £16 worth of harness, in tolerably good repair for the purpose. This was a private affair, but later Government generously repaid the cheque. In consequence, to the wonder of Frome, four gun teams turned out harnessed to some weird guns, 95-centimetre, sent over from France. The other Brigades were not slow to visit Moses; so that by April, 1915, Brigadier General Bethell's 25th Divisional Artillery could ride and drive. Their enthusiasm was great when in the spring at Winchester they were able to show their prowess to Authority. Authority said they had done wonders, but he'd rather have seen some steady marching drill. This rather dashed the younger officers' enthusiasm, until Oswald cheered them up by saying it was a way we had in the Army.

As authority perhaps gave kudos to some sister divisions who were no further than the steady marching drill stage, perhaps authority had to justify its approval there when it realised that here in the 25th Divisional Artillery was much more advanced work going on, under equal if not greater disadvantages; considering that the 25th was the more immature division. It was good luck to be so forward so early, as many a life must have later been saved by the added technical skill the 25th were able to reach.

Horses and mules, when first handled, may be a bit wild, but the sooner they are handled, especially if tired from a long journey and hungry and thirsty, the sooner they know their drivers for their friends and saviours. So in Rawalpindi in 1886; in Dehra Dun in 1907; in the Tochi Valley in 1898, when recruits and remounts came up to a sadly depleted No. 6 Jacobs Mountain Battery (see note 5); finally in 1914-15 at Frome animals were handled at once; tired and hungry, they got into grateful companionship with their new masters, young raw recruits, who had none of the experience of old-time drivers, but who found their new charges exceedingly anxious to love them—cupboard love, but to mix metaphors, it at once broke the ice. In 1914-15 there was no harness, only ropes and halters; in former years saddles and all the paraphernalia were to hand. So in 1914-15 the task was very severe. The riding began with two lessons to raw officers, who were then told to teach, with promptings from the few old soldiers, a very few, who existed. The riding school was a field and soft falling. For some days, even a month, bare back and halter rope were the only aids to horsemanship. The men were in blue uniform improvised from pre-war stocks, but they were getting on with it, so that the arrival of service dress and saddles and bits became as the dawn of luxury. All did brave and good work; falling off became a harmless act, and "hands" were formed, as they were not in use to hang on to a non-existent bit. It was a glorious example of how the British spirit will muddle through with good will and optimism everywhere. May God bless those gallant men, those volunteer soldiers, wheresoever they are in this world or the next.

Those of them who were gunner recruits had the same experiences with horses and in the mountain batteries with mules, but in a less intensified way, as their work was confined mostly to grooming, watering and riding for exercise when drivers were short. But to the

gunner recruits all the science of gunnery had
to be gradually imparted. The teachers were
content to let each gunner learn his little part
on the gun: the most intelligent as layers, that
is the pointers of the gun, the remainder as
loaders or as fuze setters, a most important
matter where shrapnel shell have to be burst
just ahead of one's own infantry and where a
badly set time-fuze may mean that bullets from
it burst in one's own advancing infantry. The
numerous duties of gunners had to be learned,
one man keeping to one roll, and to be inten-
sively trained in it alone; afterwards all parts
became familiar, but it took time to teach the
one role thoroughly. Then there was entrench-
ing. In India in 1886 this was a minor matter,
as Burmese warfare meant mainly stockade
fighting and short ranges in the jungles; in 1907
the matter had become more serious, and the
10-pounder mountain gun had to be protected
with sand bags and earthwork. By 1914-15 the
trench lines were spreading over Europe and
Asia; so the fact that many a gunner was also
a miner made this work of much interest to the
112th Brigade and others. The landowners of
Frome gave of their fields, and trenches were
dug, caverns burrowed and roofed with railway
sleepers and logs. The miners did not, it is
confessed, like the Artillery patterns of pick or
of spade, but use was everything and much was
learnt that was useful later.

The new officers in 1914-15 had a very hard

time; scientific gunnery of the 1914 pattern, signalling, map reading, reconnaissance and some military law, to mention salient items.   In scientific gunnery the study of each weapon and its powers—roughly called calibration—was a tenet in the heavier natures of guns, but had not been taken up in the R.F.A., whose accuracy of fire depended entirely on being able to see where their shell burst and fell.   Later calibration and unseen firing became possible, but in early 1915 the object of a successful battery commander was to get where he could see results of his fire.   It came to this, therefore, that nearly all the new officers were practically useless for this work when first they went to France and heavy exposure and long hours devolved on the few experienced and reliable officers who could observe what their shells were doing.   In other ways it was extraordinary how the new officers got on, but all 1915 one said, "Thank God for the British Navy."

Thanks to the "Moses" harness spoken of above, the trek from Frome to Heytesbury, to Winchester Downs, to Ewshot in Aldershot were made under march conditions, the horses dragging the old 95-centimetre guns and such supply wagons as had been collected.   The wives of officers and some others followed. Meta Williamson Oswald with the little Praxeda and Ingleby and the baby Alethea in charge of Mrs Hughes, followed first to a farm in Heyts-

bury on the edge of Salisbury Plain, then to
Compton Down, Winchester, and finally to
Fleet, Hampshire, where last days were spent,
cut into by a visit by Oswald to Annequin and
Cuinchy in Flanders in June, 1915.   In Fleet
their grandmother, Mrs Estcourt-Oswald, and
their aunt, Theodora Combe, came and saw the
children.   War makes meetings very hard to
achieve, and this was the only chance the children had of seeing their grandmother, Minnie
Estcourt-Oswald.   She was much pleased with
their manners and their accents, a point which
is easily neglected when children are young and
are liable to copy ayahs, nurses, anyone rather
than their parents.

Equipment came in fast, and Aldershot saw
the completed 25th Division of all arms—which
entrenched and manœuvred mostly in the direction of Bagshot.   Major-General Doran, Royal
Irish, an old friend, was Divisional Commander.
Bethell was C.R.A. with Oldham as Brigade
Major, Falconer Medical Officer, and Edwards
as Staff Captain.   Cloete, a horse artilleryman,
commanded one R.F.A. Brigade.   Victor Kuper,
an old friend of D Battery 4th Brigade days,
had the ammunition column, and the two R.G.A.
Lt.-Colonels, Oswald and Comyn, and another
commanded the three other R.F.A. Brigades.
So it remained in France and Belgium till
Oswald and Comyn went back to R.G.A. work,
as the field gunners became more numerous and
heavy gunners were increasingly wanted.

CHAPTER 7.

BELGIUM.

THE Sector the 25th Division had at first can roughly be called Ploegsteert—Plugstreet in the vernacular. This the Division took over about the last week of September, 1915, and stayed there till about the first week of February, 1916. The 112th Brigade R.F.A., with Oswald, had the right or southern four-gun positions and marched from Caestre through Bailleul—Baloo in the vernacular—by the pavée road as far as Nieppe and then to Le Bizet, where the houses about 4000 yards or less from the German lines were a swarming mass of Belgian women and children; amongst these houses the Infantry, not in the front trenches, rested. The conditions seem strange now, but at the time the same population close up was customary both in Armentières, the next Divisional Sector to southward, and in Annequin and other places further along towards Loos.

The guns were raging at Loos and the rain was pouring down as the 112th Brigade R.F.A. detrained at Caestre and marched its first march in France. Next day was fine, but rations came not. Probably the conditions were too much for the ration people, who had not yet much experience. Oswald hopped on a car going to Hazebrouck and made a liaison with his supply people, who played up well; but for some days rations were always on the late side. Considering this theoretically no harm was done; but as the soldier often prefers to nibble at his "unconsumed" portion of the ration, as it is humourously called, to the trouble of carrying it, so with new troops it is always as well to remember this and to make an issue 24 hours earlier than is theoretically necessary. It is not known, for instance, why the 24th Division, as described by Frankau, during the advance on Loos, were so hungry; but the "unconsumed" ration may not have been there to consume.

Orders came at Pradelles for the advance parties and Commanding Officers to go to Divisional Headquarters about 12 miles away at the Chateau of Nieppe. Nothing was said about the guns. Harold Vincent was left with the main body and the guns, and warned to pick up the rations not yet in from Hazebrouck and be ready to jump off to follow the advance parties and perhaps go into action at a moment's notice. He did not get his rations before he moved, but wisely left sufficient transport to bring on the rations, which turned up that afternoon with that day's food, and caught up the batteries in action. As regards the move

of the guns, on arrival at Divisional Headquarters, the plan was disclosed that they were
to go into action that night; this to be fair had
been intended to be part of the original movement order, but had not been included, and they
were some 12 miles away. Luckily it was possible to buzz off a motor cyclist to Harold
Vincent and all was well. It is in relation to
this incident, and others of a similar but not so
fortunate a nature, that all his service the sight
of the red hat or its equivalent has always
acted on Oswald's subconscious mind as creat-
ing a premonition. This premonition has
caused the instantaneous thought: now something will have to be done for which there
is really not enough time. When there is
enough time the order comes along peacefully
and quietly in the shape of the post-orderly with
a letter. Let red hats and brass hats mark this.
In 1915 we were very young.

The headquarters* of the 112th Brigade
R.F.A. were in a farm on the Wanave River,
or rather deep ditch about 3 yards broad at the
waterline, which was about 4 feet below the
level of the surrounding fields of low-lying
Flanders. The men, telephonists, clerks, and
others were in the farm barn where the telephone exchange was. The officers were in the
living room and a small annexe. The farmer
and family were in the cellar for sleeping and
the kitchen by day, which the brigade also used.
It was not the brigade battle headquarters.

---

*See Sketch opposite Title Page.

These were somewhat better defended, being in
a semi-underground basement about a mile and
a half nearer the front in Belgian Le Bizet village, where the Infantry Brigade defending this
sector also had its battle headquarters.   The
mud at the farm was very bad for digging
trenches, but still on the experience of after
years it was a very exposed position.   This was
indeed shown one day during a ranging trial,
or registration (see explanation page 200) of
the farm by German field howitzers, 4.2-inch,
when the only place to turn to for shelter was
behind a small haystack near the farm, an
inadequate defence, and one which left the telephone exchange exposed.   It would have been
better to have faced the mud and water and
dug down a bit in the fields near the farm.
However, there was a certain touchiness about
digging so far back from the line in those days.
A compromise was effected later by Oswald,
who prospected and arranged to lead a line into
the Warnave ditch near the farm, so that the
telephone could remain in action even if the
farm were destroyed.   The registration of the
farm by the enemy's shells, or colloquially the
measuring by trial shots so as to hit the farm,
if necessary, ceased when the enemy were satisfied they could hit the farm.

No sooner was it over than one officer went
off to locate some shell holes, collect souvenirs
and identify what shells had made them.   Unfortunately the shelling started again round

him and he had to leg it, followed by laughter from the unsympathetic audience.

Talking of touchiness, one event that always seemed to draw the Corps Headquarters was a report of sniping behind the trenches.   This was natural, as the whole policy was to assume the greatest loyalty among all the inhabitants; but mysterious happenings occurred.   For instance, one gloaming a bang in what seemed the small of Oswald's back as he was walking home to the billet, followed by a tinkling of tiles from the billet's outhouses led to a rush of men to the rescue.   However, there was a good deal of cover along the Warnave ditches and nothing came of it, nor was anyone found out.

The four brigades of the R.F.A. 25th Division were strung along the line, a frontage from Le Bizet on the Belgian-French Frontier to the far, or north, end of Ploegsteert Wood towards Messines with Ypres beyond.   This meant that each 18-pr. brigade held about a mile's frontage (see note 3) at a range of about $1\frac{3}{4}$ to $2\frac{1}{4}$ miles from the German front trenches and was in support of one Infantry brigade.   The fourth R.F.A. Brigade were 4.5-inch howitzers, four four-gun batteries as were all the brigades. These howitzers were distributed to cover the whole divisional front.   An incident, that showed how raw the troops were, occurred when one howitzer battery was asked to destroy some German works which were made of thick logs and which were too strong for the

18-pound shells. Ammunition was very limited, and only about 50 rounds were asked for. These were fired, but by means of the map and without any correction by personal observation by the howitzer battery officers. Campbell of the 18-pr. battery who wanted the work done, had he been asked, could easily have corrected the firing, which unfortunately just missed the mark. So much for want of experience.

The trenches were full of water and mud and had to be pumped out. Troops wore India-rubber waders coming nearly to the thigh all the winter of 1915-16. The pictures by Bairns-father give an exact presentment of the front and areas behind. It was close to Armentières, which held the next or southward Division. This place was spared at that time by the Germans, who could easily have wrecked it, and was full of people, cafés and estaminets. Later in 1918 it was drenched with poison gas. That this sparing of places was not meant for sparing of troops can be judged by the following. The 25th Division arranged some hot water baths in Belgian Le Bizet. These were a great luxury; often a soldier got a hot water bath there as frequently as at 3 weeks' interval during the winter of 1915-16. Here also lousy garments were cleaned, or if too bad were changed, but this part of the line having been made by British and kept British was not so lousy as some other sectors. Unfortunately, some inexperienced officer took his men to the

baths in some sort of ostentatious march formation one day, and then crowded them in the
courtyard of the mill where the baths were. A
German plane saw this and the German 5.9-inch
heavy guns, from somewhere on the right bank
of the Lys, wrecked the divisional baths so
severely that they had to be moved, and the
troops in Le Bizet had a long trudge of a
further three miles to Nieppe before they could
get a good bath.

As the winter came on, cover to hide the
guns got hard to arrange, as they had been
mainly hidden by the foliage of willow trees and
hedgerows. The cover was now the bare sticks
of the trees and shrubs. With horror then the
troops saw the Belgians commence to prune
their pollarded willows of the bare branches,
and the corps and the division were asked to
interfere, which they did. It is presumed they
got compensation, as payment* was made for
all billets, fields used for horse lines, and, it was
said, for the ground used for training too. The
horse lines were never changed, as it was hoped
that so far to the rear, some 4 or 5 miles back
from the front trenches, most of the fields would
be cultivated or grazed, as indeed they were.
The fields where the horses were crowded consequently got churned up into a mixture of mud,
water and horse litter. The straw, hay and
grain were preserved as much as possible, but
some naturally mixed with the mud. This mud
was some three feet deep, and when the horses

*by governments to their own nationals,

were led out for work or exercise they were a plaster of muck, which drivers somehow had to clean off. Batteries were always clamouring for bricks to make some sort of platform for the horse standings to keep the animals out of the mud. The same troubles had occurred in 1885 on Khanna Plain at Rawalpindi, India, when Oswald was mobilised against Russia with P. Field Battery 3rd Brigade R.A. as a Lieutenant (see Chapter 3). There, luckily, Russia and England composed their differences, and the martyrdom of the horses only lasted a few weeks.

Bricks, it will be understood, meant the saving of the horses' lives in this muddy part of Flanders; but often bricks were not. However, the R.A. Staff of the division had a keen ear, and batteries were quietly informed where brick harvests lay. Hoping against hope the various gallant Civil Mayors and other functionaries of Belgian and French villages refused to allow a brick to be moved from any of the ruined houses or other buildings, unless they could certify it was a portion of a building actually destroyed by the enemy's action and so to be paid for when peace came. One such case of destruction among many occurred amongst a few workmen's houses, and the Functionary agreed to certify the buildings destroyed. For this purpose he went down to the place about noon the following day. He found to his astonishment there were no houses to be certi-

fied; for every brick had been spirited away by
eager drivers since dawn, when his verbal
certification of the previous night began to be
acted upon; such was the hunger for bricks to
save the poor horses from standing in mud.   It
is believed the French paid for all bricks used.

The usual fighting went on day after day,
month after month, with a steady trickle of
losses, and a steady trickle of Germans who
showed up, taking short cuts from trench to
trench, or who were otherwise careless of life.
The O.P.'s of the four batteries, or observation
posts, varied.   One was in the eaves of a tiled
house in a long ruined street in the village of
Le Touquet, opposite Frelinghein on the river
Lys below Armentières.   Le Touquet was a
shell of a village.   From house to house
wriggled a trench and curiously enough even a
light railway, which in parts was hidden or
camouflaged by a sort of canvas tent; this railway had a terminus about three hundred yards
from the front trenches, which here were not
more than ten yards from the Germans.

Inside, the observation posts were much
alike.   A table, a map, reports and, perched
above, the observer could be seen in the arti-
ficial gloom made by a piece of sacking or
blanket.   This screen hid all of the peepholes
or cracks through which the observer was able
to observe, except the small portion he had in
use at the time, while generally behind him
there was placed a second screen to prevent any

outline to be seen from the enemy's side.
Generally also the powerful battery telescope
upon its stand was worked by the observer. It
had a plate graduated in degrees and minor
divisions, so that the direction of any object
could be located with reference to the north and
so be observable on the battery maps. This
eyrie was always placed as high in the air as
safety from the enemy's sight allowed. Safety
from fire, even from a stray bullet, and certainly from a chance shell, there was in most
cases none at all up there with the observer.
Safety gradually began at the table where the
maps were. This safety was day by day pain-
fully acquired as sandbags arrived and could
be filled and built up through one or two stories
of crazy ruined rooms. Sandbags, corrugated
iron, and timber made these defences. Thanks
were given by many to the public-spirited Miss
Tyler, who asked the women of England to sew
sacking into sandbags, in spite of protests from
Authority that there was no need to do it. At
any rate Miss Tyler's sandbags got filled and
built up into many a hefty wall.

One battery observation post was up a
chimney, and in this case luckily a few sandbags
were possible to defend the observer. Luckily,
for it is bad to lose men in time of indecisive
trench warfare, and here the Germans were
rather fond of shrapneling the chimney, but did
not hit it except with bullets, which the sandbags stopped. The third battery observation

post was in the roof of a high ruined barn; here as elsewhere the telephonists were as low down as possible and dug into a shelter, but could hear the observer's words, though sometimes a man had to be posted in between telephone and observer to pass ranges, orders and messages. This observation post then was very exposed, a stage held the table and maps—a stage built on 20-feet high legs—while up above it in the roof was a ladder to hold another small and dusty-looking platform with peepholes through the tiles and the best view of the trenches, and even No Man's Land some 1200 yards in front towards the Lys at Warneton. This No Man's Land, though not so narrow as at the Lys at Le Touquet, was only about 60 to 100 yards wide along the front of the 25th Division. Owing to the swampy ground, the defences on both sides stood up some three to eight feet above the level of the fields and were composed on the British side of a wall of mud and sandbags and on the German side of sandbags of many colours, caused by their composition, which seemed to be of materials such as bed clothing and mattresses brought from the neighbourhood. In front of the sandbags was a continuous belt of barbed wire, red and brown from rust, and a thicket of wire, on an average ten feet thick and some three to five feet high. The British barbed wire was of one or two strands, and that usually seen in England, with a spike at about every foot or under. The

German wire looked like a thick briar rose or
blackberry branch and was of four or five
strands, and seemed to have spikes at every six
inches or so, while it was about half an inch in
diameter, and so hard to cut with wire cutters.
Between the two rows of barbed wire were
dank and rotting patches of green grass and
weeds and of brown earth; while here and there
were pools of water and holes half filled with
water and the black slime from bursting shells
which had ploughed up the ground and made
these holes or shell craters, as they were named.
There were some tree stumps nearly flush with
the ground, bits of rags that had been clothes,
and after a night skirmish sometimes a body or
two till opportunity for salvage was possible,
when one side or the other took it in; the object
of the salvage being either to bring in a com-
rade's body, or to identify from the uniform
what regiment of the enemy lay in front. This
identification business was very necessary and
precious, but sometimes not quite reliable, as
when a unit "identified" the same regiment
night after night and was quite annoyed when
some busybody brought in the "data" on which
the identification was made and buried it; however this was not the 25th Division.

The fourth Battery's observation post was
a small porter's lodge or some such building of
two stories. The upper one was screened
somewhat by trees, and the observer looked
through a screened window. A comfortable

post to sit in; unfortunately it was on a cart track marked on maps and directly leading enemywards, so that the Germans sprayed this track with machine gun bullets at odd hours, or constantly, and many bullets came into the observer's window.   The alternative window in the lower storey therefore became used when observation from there was possible, as the machine-gun bullets could not impinge upon it so easily owing to the configuration of the ground, while observation was still well above the surrounding land.

The front trenches were used for observing shell fired for cutting the enemy's barbed wire. An observer had to use a periscope or to put his head up high enough to see the barbed wire. The latter was best, but became too deadly to be indulged in for a long period, so was only used for an instant to correct the fine shooting necessary to hit the wire once the exact range had been found, and then if possible the head was not always raised from the same place.   A periscope in those days was a rough affair of two looking-glasses, one fixed on a stick or other upright and the other below the parapet, into which shone the reflexion of the upper mirror and the view it gave of the enemy's wire or other objective.   The fault was that the mirrored view was very small and gave no idea of real size or distance; hence the necessity of looking over the parapet with raised head. Later much better telescopic periscopes were

provided. Oswald by good fortune possessed
a two-eyed telescope made by Zeiss of Jena,
which he had used for some years as a periscope
as well as a telescope. It came in very handy,
as though only 6 inches from eye-piece to view-
piece or object glass, this was enough to hide
the head, while the view was a fine telescopic
one of great power.

So training and fighting went on hand in
hand; experiments, some practical, some weird,
were made in order to break down the German
defence, but the forces were too equal, and as
in past wars between equals the trenches were
to be the battlefields for years. In 1916 Oswald
left the 112 Brigade R.F.A., with many warm
remembrances for good comrades.

CHAPTER 8.

AFTER leaving the 112th Brigade R.F.A., Oswald went to the front south of Arras, and in March, 1916 commanded 19th Heavy Artillery Group until April, 1916, when he was transferred to Bordon Camp near Aldershot as Commandant. These transfers increased his knowledge of all natures of guns, as 19th H.A.G., or Heavy Artillery Group, was a siege group having 6-inch, 8-inch, 9.2-inch and 15-inch (marine artillery) howitzers with some counter-battery duties. This part of the front was recently taken over from the French. There was a rumour that the German sniper dominated some of the line hereabouts where the hostile trenches each ran not quite on the top ridge of the dividing neutral ground. The dominance was said to be due to the Germans not having observed a "tacit" understanding to leave the crest alone. The story is given for what it is worth. At any rate with the arrival of the British things livened up, and the Germans no longer dominated the crest line and the allied trenches.

This period of change from France to

Bordon seems to be a chance to describe how
for long years Oswald was mixed up in the
British effort to obtain better artillery, especially artillery for modern war; how in his own
case the effort centralised round the production
of guns worthy to arm the British and Indian
Mountain Artillery, and culminated in the
production of Mountain guns of a worthy type
and fit to take part in the great struggle of 1914
to 1920. The story is, unfortunately, technical
in parts, but it is also dramatic, as the successful guns were made just in time for the great
struggle.

In 1880, at Christmas, Oswald became a
soldier. During two years he drilled, studied
and served practically as a soldier in barracks,
being first cadet and then Corporal. Six
months as a young officer was devoted to more
advanced work in the science of the Army, and
especially of the Artillery arm. It so happened
that from 1883 till 1906 he never had a theoretical lesson in the art of war from paid teachers,
though, of course, he had plenty in the field and
at manœuvres and at Artillery practice camps.
In 1906 he studied by correspondence with the
United Service Institution staff at Simla and
passed for Lt.-Colonel, since when military
professional examinations have not been required from him. He studied by himself for
his Captain's and Major's examinations and for
one shot at the Staff College. At the Staff
College entrance he made 88 per cent. marks in

tactics and did fairly well in other subjects, but failed to pass by 12 marks in French. He thought, perhaps wrongly, that he was not linguist enough to get a pass into the College among the very limited vacancies allowed to artillery officers, and so diverted his attention to practical gunnery as a regimental officer. This was in 1892.

From 1880 things had been in a curious position in British gunnery. At that time the British, both Army and Navy, were committed to the theory that muzzle-loading guns were preferable to breach-loading guns.   There existed in those days the Armstrong breech-loading guns. The shells were coated with lead and the guns had numerous grooves cut inside their bores, and the result was a number of satisfactory weapons of fair accuracy, from guns of 7 inches width of bore to those of about 3 inches width. The breech or back-end of these guns was closed with a heavy steel block which was let down into place behind the loaded cartridge and then pushed forward by means of a screwing up arrangement in the gun. Occasionally the lead which coated the shells was torn off when the shell rushed out of the bore of the gun as the grooves of rifling endeavoured to do their duty of giving a spin to the shell, and there was trouble, a short shell perhaps falling among friendly soldiers; or the loose lead coating doing damage. But this did not often happen. However, both Navy and

Army magnates, who had to decide on British guns, decided to put aside the Armstrong guns and to get a rifled muzzle-loading type. The shells, instead of being lead-coated, had about nine brass knobs put on their cylindrical sides in about three rows: these knobs fitted into grooves cut into the inside of the gun and cut on a twist. The shells were loaded after the cartridge had been loaded, both from the front end, or muzzle end of the gun. A hole was bored into the gun at the hinder end, and by that means the gun was fired. The knobs on shells then took a twisting motion from the twisting spiral of the grooves cut in the bore of the gun and the shell went on its way point first, spinning like a rifle bullet and with some accuracy. It is a fact that this spin gives accuracy. As the big guns fired they gradually developed great cuts in the inside of the bore, as the powder gas rushed out, some of it escaping between the shell and the bore of the gun. However, this was the sort of weapon the Navy, in 1883, and the Army till after 1885, had to put up with. The field Artillery of that day had practically a shrapnel range of about 1800 yards only—say, a mile.

Those in power must have been uneasy, as experiments in muzzle loaders went on, and instead of the shells with brass knobs on them, or " studded projectiles " as they were called, a new pattern of shell was invented for the muzzle-loading guns. This pattern had a brass saucer fixed on the bottom end of the shell, and the saucer being comparatively soft, jambed itself on the shell when the powder blast of firing struck it, while the saucer's edge being soft, got into the spiral grooves, cut into the inside of the bore of the gun, and so gave a twisting rifled motion to the shell when fired. The saucer certainly acted better than the " studded projectile " method, as it more or less prevented the wasteful and destroying rush of the powder gas past the shell after firing.   It was, therefore, called a gas check.   This arrangement existed in some natures of guns for many years, certainly until the middle nineties, while with black powder the mountain gunners fought with gas check guns in 1900 in South Africa.   They were considered an out-of-date nuisance by many, and so failed to get that prestige the mountain or pack Artillery considers it deserves as the close up Artillery weapon.

Consider, then, that all these years, and even in 1883, every other nation had discarded their muzzle-loading guns as well as their muzzle-loading rifles, and imagine a scientific instructor of gunnery trying to explain away the out-of-date weapons of the British in 1883 to a squad of young officers of Artillery just commissioned and going through a course of Artillery at Shoeburyness.   Fortunately for the Artillery Instructor there was at Shoeburyness one better gun.   This was a 12-pounder field gun with a breech made on the French "De Bange" principal, one which closed the breech in a satisfactory manner by means of asbestos discs which, working between metal or gun metal discs, squeezed the asbestos so as to prevent the rush of powder gas over the breech screw when the gun was fired. This gun was shown to the class as the gun of the future, and its mechanism for safely closing a breech-loading gun has lasted with some guns till now. The breech screw was made to push into place, and then with a turn of a portion of a circle, the teeth of the screw locked with teeth inside the breech of the gun and so took the shock of firing. The firing was arranged for either by means of a cap, much on the lines of a shot gun, or by means of an electric current, which fired a small charge, which, in turn, fired the cartridge. The cartridges were made of strong silk and contained powder, or smokeless powder, as invention progressed. This smokelessness is a comparative term only, and depends in degree on light and other causes. The electric current was mainly used for naval and stationary guns: it is very rapid in action, allowing a quick rate of fire, but has been accused of being the cause of fatal accidents. The accusation is that it is not fool-proof, as it allows of a dangerous adjustment. This adjustment is arranged for by allowing the electric contact to take place before the breech part of the gun is safely closed. There is a margin of safety in the normal adjustment; should this be slightly altered, all is still safe, but the gun goes off perhaps the fifth of a second earlier, which is advantageous, but very risky, in competitions. Should this adjustment, however, get slightly displaced, the cartridge fires before the breech is properly closed. So died many good Artillery Officers and men at Freshwater, Isle of Wight, in the nineties.

The use of the silk cloth cartridge case to hold the powder, now generally cordite, had an unforeseen advantage in the war of 1914 to 1918. When copper began to be scarce, those nations, particularly the Central European Powers, Germany and Austria, and their subordinates, Bulgaria and Turkey, who almost exclusively used brass cases to hold the powder for their guns, found there was not enough copper to supply their wants. Britain, who had avoided copper for her larger guns, found that her call for brass cartridge cases was, in consequence, kept in limits. The object of brass cartridge cases was quickness in loading and firing the gun, especially the field gun. The shell and cartridge in these cases were, in consequence, joined together and looked like a gigantic rifle cartridge. These shells and cartridges could, therefore, be loaded in one motion, a great advantage for quickness.

The larger shells could not load with their cartridge, as they were too heavy, so in their case it mattered not whether the cartridge was in a brass or a silk case, so far as quickness in loading went. The brass of the cartridge case was, however, further utilised to act as part of the gun; it did so by helping to close securely the breech end. This simplified the building of the gun, but not to a great degree, and the asbestos pads or discs, where used by the French and British, closed the breech just as effectively without the extra complication of having brass cartridge cases for the bigger guns. Imagine in a battle also the tremendous litter behind every field gun and other guns using brass cartridge cases. As the firing goes on, after each shot is fired, the gun is opened to receive one more round of shell and brass cartridge, and as the breech mechanism opens for this purpose, out from the smoking gun springs the cartridge case of brass which has just fired. As these brass cases fall out of the gun they make a heap on the ground round the feet of the men working at the gun. When possible, some one clears them away, but often in a hot fight there is no chance to clear the cases away, while in a retreat much valuable brass has to be left to the enemy. It was, therefore, a decided advantage from this point of view that Britain was not entirely dependent on copper for their gun cartridge cases, but could in some cases use silk. Silk cartridge bags, it will be realised, left no litter, nor had they to be cleared from the guns after firing, as the slik was completely gone when fired.

A big reform in Field and Mountain Artillery had to come after 1883 before these natures of guns could fire really quickly, so as to profit by the inventions referred to in the previous sentences. For years before 1883 the guns were stationary in the forts and navies of the world, to speak colloquially. In these forts and ships the guns could not be allowed to bound backwards without control when fired. There was no room for this bounding backwards. When Oswald joined, and indeed in some of the Portsmouth Forts as late as 1892, there were to be found these old-fashioned guns and carriages. The old 32-pound round shot or cannon ball of Nelson's days was fired in his times from a smooth-bored muzzle-loading gun which sat on a wooden carriage with wheels about one foot in diameter to support it in front, and, so far as can be traced, with wheels or flat blocks of wood to support the wooden carriage elsewhere. The gun went off and bounded back with its wooden carriage. It was controlled by ropes and tackle to the extent such material would allow, which was not very much. After the bound or recoil, the gun was laboriously levered and pushed back into its place. True, the 32-pound round shot had gone before the eighties; a 64-pound conical shell had replaced it, which was attained and made possible by strengthening the old gun of Nelson's days, and by boring the inside of the gun so that it became a rifled gun.

In fort and navy a reform had come in the 1870's, namely, so to anchor the gun carriage that it did not move about when the gun was fired.   On this fixed portion slid up and down the gun and a sort of upper carriage.   This upper carriage was in danger of bounding off the under carriage or gun slide, but a buffer, somewhat in the nature of a railway buffer, was arranged to join the bounding part to the fixed part, and so it does unto this day.   In field guns invention halted, and the nations had field-gun carriages which bounded about, more or less.   The British 18-pounder gun was invented, and bounded rather less than more.   This was after 1900 and the South African War.   It was, therefore, possible to stand behind the 18-pounder gun and load and fire without danger of being crushed by a bounding gun and carriage.   This led to another invention for field gunners.   This was a steel shield on the carriage, behind which the gunners could shelter their bodies from fire coming from an enemy in front.   As regards any other fire, of course, shelter could be constructed of earth, sand in sandbags, and so on, as the problem of a bounding gun did not enter in.

It was into this problem of protection and gun power that Oswald was at this time brought personally.   Before the South African War Oswald was a captain in command of an Indian Mountain Battery, or rather various batteries; temporarily of the 1 Kohat, 7 Bengal,

4 Hazara, and the stationary battery in Kohat
Fort, nicknamed " the Blokes." Ultimately, in
1897, No. 6 Jacob's Mountain Battery became
vacant.   All this time Oswald was either
winning shooting competitions or having a try
for them, which is the common and salutary lot
of gunners.   He had a good and expensive
equipment of field glasses made by Zeiss of
Jena, then in the forefront of telescope and field
glass inventors and makers, mainly because
Zeiss had developed the principal of Prismatic
Lenses for vision.   The power of field glasses
required for field and mountain guns in those
days was not for very long range; about 2000
yards for mountain guns, though 3000—say,
2 miles—was expected occasionally. Gone were
the days of firing bundles of bullets called
" case shot " out of a funny soda-water bottle
shaped piece of artillery, weighing 200 pounds,
muzzle-loading, and all in one piece, which
firing a 7-pound shell up to, say, 1500 yards, or
a weird double shell up to 800 or 1000 yards, was
the weapon still in use in the jungle frontiers
of Burma in 1897.   This one-piece muzzle-
loader was a survival deliberately retained for
jungle fighting, but it was soon obsolete or
obsolescent.   Its excuse was simplicity and
quickness; but it had to go before the demand
for more powerful guns.   Its successor was the
screw-gun—that is, a piece built in two pieces;
and so, while weighing 400 pounds, it could be
carried upon the backs of two mules, while it

provided a gun twice the length of the 200-pound gun, and was a good accurate gun for well over 2000 yards—say, 1½ miles of range. It was invented about 1880, fought in various wars up till 1904; but it was a muzzle-loader and burnt black powder, which, as has been said, gave it away both on the Indian Frontier and in South Africa in 1900, causing the infantry who were firing smokeless powder to avoid its neighbourhood, and making staffs and generals curse its presence as giving their dispositions away to the enemy.

In 1894, while fighting in Waziristan, Oswald also was fortunate enough to win for No. 1 Kohat Mountain Battery the third place in prize shooting amongst all the Mountain batteries in India, British and Native; he was ably assisted by the Subalterns, Money, Hudson and Seagrim. He took advantage of his position, and was backed up by Captain, the late Brigadier-General, J. L. Parker, R.A. of the Peshawar Mountain Battery, a fiery and highly trained gunner. This officer never minced matters. An example may be given: Gatacre, nicknamed Back-acher, with a good record, was tackled on the subject of an ill-considered move of Parker's battery, and Gatacre's staff had to acknowledge the inferior staff work which left, so 'tis said, Parker's battery and its escort rationless upon a mountain pass and in its adjacent camps, in one of which the High Command found them, and thereby the story arose that Parker had reported his General. After the incident of Stormberg, South Africa, where Gatacre commanded, Parker somewhat grimly remarked: " Perhaps there was some right on the side of whoever reported Gatacre." (See note 4). This quality of Parker's, of not minimising matters, gave a powerful help to the protest of the mountain gunners about the ineffectiveness of the muzzle-loading screw-gun. At a camp in the Tochi Valley, about 1899, the very efficient Artillery umpires criticised some of the shooting, giving as the cause the inferior laying—that is, gun point-ing—of the men. Parker said, " No men can be better trained; it is not humanly possible. You must look elsewhere for the cause of inaccurate guns." True enough, with advancing science, Artillerymen have learnt to look further, to realise that even with the lighter guns such causes as the wear of the bore and the barometric pressure are reasons for changes in the fall of the shell; but the main cause at the time, in 1899, when Parker spoke up, was a long-dated want for a new and more modern Mountain gun.

With 1904, a new gun arrived—the 10-pounder breech-loader firing smokeless powder. It was a good gun; but the Field Artillery were then evolving a gun which had a spade and buffers to prevent its recoil, and a real quick-firing field gun was envisaged that would not bound about when fired.   On his first parade

with this new 10-pounder, Oswald said to
Parsons, the new Inspector General of Artillery
in India, now we must get a quick-firing
Mountain gun with a shield. Oswald had
served in the South African War in 1901, and
as Parsons was there as well, the request was
favourably criticised, though Parsons said:
"You fellows are never content. You just
have a brand new gun here." "Yes," said
Oswald; "but it is not good enough." His
battery was the remarkable No. 5 Mountain
R.G.A., lately commanded by that Master of
Mountain Guns, Fogarty Fegan; the Captain
was Owen; the subalterns were Hall, Loveday
and Barker; later Hutton-Squire, Cameron and
Erskine; there were also Sergeant-Major Carey
and Quartermaster-Sergeant Wright, with a
galaxy of Sergeants and non-commissioned
officers and men, whose destiny was, in many
cases, to become officers in the Great War.

This formidable instrument showed the
power of the new 10-pounder in many severe
tests from 1904 to 1906, when Oswald went to
Simla and Calcutta as an attaché to Indian
Army Headquarters (Kitchener's). (See
Note 26). The Royal Garrison Artillery at
that time had the advantage over the Field that
their men, before becoming Mountain gunners,
had trained with real quick-firing guns. Their
weapons were the fixed quick-firers which
armed the forts in the coast defence. These
guns were the last word in science, and could

squirt shells as through a hose. The 12-pounder quick-firer could fire 15 shells in one minute. Oswald had had the inestimable advantage of service with his South African Battery, 98 Company R.G.A., in Halifax, Canada. This was a North Irish Battery. Halifax was an up-to-date fortress bristling with heavy guns and quick-firers. His Colonel, Rigg; his captains, Phillipps, Rambaut, and Gordon; subalterns, L. Galloway, Gee, and Matterson; Morgan had been left in South Africa. The Sergeant-Major was Tyler. Some records were scored at practice here in 1902 and 1903.

The main effect of all this was that though the 10-pounder was a weapon that bounded when it fired, still its R.G.A. gun crews were imbued with the quick-firing spirit, and some astonishingly rapid and accurate fire was produced first by No. 5 Moutain Battery, and then by others at the same camp, while the artillery who had fired with a new light field gun, which was supposed to be a quick-firer, were given food for thought as to possibilities of squirting death. In short, what with one thing and another, the quick-firing spirit began to permeate the ranks of all artillerymen in India; and by 1912, when 18-pounders had become the weapon of the field artillery, some astonishingly good and quick shooting was the rule, and this bore fruit in the Great War, 1914 to 1918.

The 10-pounder Mountain Gun struggled on;

it came into action in various small wars, including for Oswald the Persian Expedition of 1911 (see note 5) against the Afghan Gilzai gun-smugglers, gun-runners as they were called. Light in the darkness of using so obsolete a gun was coming. About 1906 Dowell and Knapp, two experienced mountain battery commanders, were put on the Artillery Committee to evolve at Woolwich an up-to-date mountain gun, and, it is believed, a mountain howitzer as well. Oswald nearly went too, but reasons of expense prevented three going. This Committee did its work, but no gun came to India. Oswald then had raised 32, now Poonch, Indian Mountain Battery, Captain Swinton, Subalterns Spencer, Dowding and Maclean, Indian Officers, now Hon. Captain Mohamed Ismail, a celebrated man, Kushial Singh, Sher Baz, and a number of N.C.O.'s, including Harnam Singh, and men who fought, and many of whom became officers in the Great War. The battery was doing well, and so in 1909 Oswald went home, where his newly married wife, Meta, née Carson, had preceded him. This marriage was a great turning point in Oswald's life, and he may thank God for this great blessing.

Before departure, and as he knew he might well have been one of the originals as mentioned above to evolve a new mountain gun, Oswald asked to be attached while on his year's leave to the Artillery Committee to ferret out what was happening and why no gun had yet come to India. Army Headquarters arranged the matter, and Oswald became in 1909 the representative of the Mountain Artillery on the Artillery Committee at Woolwich.

This Committee met about fortnightly, but the Secretary, Byron, told Oswald that the question of the mountain guns would not come up so often as that. For meetings to which he was summoned Oswald got a guinea fee, his railway fare, cab fares, and expenses if he had to stay in London, when there for a night on committee work. He asked at first to attend meetings even if not summoned, and, of course, bore this expense himself. The gun now developing into the present mountain 2.75-inch gun, firing shrapnel and common shell of 10 pounds weight, was practically ready, but it had certain faults which were in course of correction.

This process of correction was a revelation to Oswald. At one of his first meetings a question of either the buckle of a strap, or the shape of some small excrescence easily altered, or some other simple point came forward. He was asked his opinion as to the suggested simple change and acquiesced. The next meeting came on; he was not summoned, but he went, and asked about the simple change.   Had it been carried out?   Oh no; why the draughtsman had not yet had it sent to him. In due course the draughtsman would make his draught sketch. This sketch then came before the committee. Some period after accepting the draught sketch a specimen model came in; later the actual alteration was put on the equipment, but the whole process had taken many weeks to perform. It is not claimed that this delay was due to any want of efficiency. The experimental machinery of the Army and Navy was limited on the score of expense, and this particular alteration on the equipment of the mountain gun had to wait its turn with that of other experimental equipments. To mention such experimental equipments as the 9.2-inch howitzer, the caterpillar tractor, and various field howitzers, will suffice to show their extreme importance.

Oswald now felt that he had received the enlightenment he required. He had learnt the reason why no new pattern mountain gun had yet gone to India, in spite of the efficient labours of Dowell and Knapp. Incidentally he had learnt why new patterns of equipment in the service were so slow in getting to the regiments and batteries. On the one side there were the financial people, not at all anxious to spend money on new armaments, while on the other there were the Services crying for up-to-date weapons. If between these there were a series of experimenters and experts, who would be satisfied with nothing but perfection; the procedure of draught sketch, model and experimental pattern, dragged out through weeks and months, played the game of the financial side and gave it respite from having to buy a new

weapon. Sometimes the experiments went on
so long that at last the new weapon was out of
date and experiments had to begin all over
again.

Oswald now announced that he accepted
the new mountain gun, called the 2.75-inch
shielded quick-firer, firing a 10-pound* shell, and
the whole of its equipment with all its minor
faults. He was of the opinion that it was fit
for the service and could be manufactured and
sent out to India. In those days there was no
Mountain Artillery in Britain except among the
Territorials. This decision he defended, as he
said that in all equipments changes of a minor
nature were continually being made while the
soldiers and sailors were actually using the
weapons, and that any wanted in the 2.75-inch
mountain gun could be taken in hand after the
gun was in the service. This decision was
endorsed. Oswald knew he ran the risk of
obloquy from gunners who would expect perfection in their new weapon and would not find it.
It was, in his opinion, a vast advance on the
bounding and recoiling 10-pounder gun. May
the fact that now in 1927, as these words are
written, the 2.75-inch is the gun of the Mountain
Artillery, speak in support of his daring
opinion?

The decision to manufacture the new pattern
mountain gun was about 1910 communicated to
the financial people of the Army in India. It
may have caused some tribulation, as the Indian

---

*or slightly heavier,

Army was being run on the principle of getting
a round sum and doing its best on it. Its financial guardians were very able men, but their
purse was by no means long enough to neglect
the extra call of a new mountain gun and
equipment for over twenty batteries. The old
game of experiment began again, in India this
time. About this time Oswald's leave in
England was over; but a year later, in 1911, he
was promoted Lt.-Colonel, R.G.A., and sent to
Golden Hill, Isle of Wight, the centre and school
of scientific gunnery, and also again resumed
sittings with the Artillery Committee. It then
transpired that the finance department in India
had ordered that only two guns were to be made
and sent out for even more experiments in
India. This would not do, so a word in season
went to India, which at last budgeted for the
necessary mountain artillery about 1912 or 1913.
These guns never came out to India, but they
were in process of being made before the Great
War began (see note 6). On the arrival in
Europe of the three mountain batteries, with
the 3rd and 7th Indian Divisions, in 1914, these
three batteries were rapidly armed with the
new shielded gun. Gradually as the war went
on all other mountain batteries discarded the
bounding 10-pounder for new shielded guns as
equipments became ready. This may be considered a successful effort to get better guns,
and luckily in time.

The 10-pounder, unshielded as it was, had

to bear the brunt of many a hard fight still.
For example, in German East Africa, the 27th
and 28th Indian Mountain Batteries had such
an experience of loss from unshielded guns that,
as Tancock or Forestier-Walker wrote and told
Oswald, they manufactured boiler-plating into
shields (see note 23) so as to obtain partial protection in action, and they also sent him some
photographs. Oswald sent on the photographs
of these shields to Goold-Adams at the War
Office in 1914, but alas, rightly or wrongly,
Adams could not move the War Office to provide
shields for the 10-pounders, as the pundits quite
truly said that shields had never been used with
recoiling guns. Perhaps the War Office saw
the better way was to get the new gun for the
mountain gunners as soon as possible.

From France and Belgium, where Oswald
met the new mountain guns with his old friend
Molesworth of No. 2 Mountain Battery in the
trenches near Ploegsteert (Plugstreet) Wood,
their mutual destiny took them to Krusha
Balkans in Macedonia in 1916 and 1917, where
No. 5, Oswald's old command, was near him.
An official visit to this battery had a great effect
on Hoar, the Medical Officer of 61 Heavy Artillery Group, whose duty it was to inspect it. He
was met with such military precision and taken
round with such smartness, and found things
in such order, that he came back much
impressed with what an old-time regular
battery of mountain artillery stood for. He

also brought the yarn that in 1905 when No. 5, under Oswald, was doing some good shooting at targets in India and gaining some of its succession of prize badges, the men of the battery always knew things were all right in action "if the Old Man's putties then came down round his ankles." Oswald thought this story a base libel.

CHAPTER 9.

THE scene of the effort to obtain good and new mountain artillery guns now changes to Palestine. The XXI. Corps are struggling for Jerusalem; the time is near the end of November, 1917. Oswald is acting as Brigadier-General, commanding the Royal Artillery of the Corps. He meets a friend near Kuryet-el-Enab, in the Judean Hills, a Sabbath day's journey from Jerusalem, as the New Testament says; this is A. Colvile, his old subaltern of 6 (Jacobs) Mountain Battery. Colvile is commanding a battery equipped with a weapon that has not yet fired in anger, but is to do great work in the struggle for Jerusalem, and to fire a hitherto unheard of shell both here and in many a fight up to the day of writing these words. This weapon is the 3.7-inch Mountain Howitzer, quick-firing, shielded, and firing a 20-pound shell loaded with high explosive to a range of 6000 yards, or $3\frac{1}{2}$ miles. A Brigade under Tancock of three batteries or twelve howitzers is destined to help in the taking of Jerusalem, and ultimately in the Turkish defeat of 1918, with its results,

95

which were, it is conjectured, felt on all fronts.

Oswald was very well pleased to meet these batteries, as their fire was going to reinforce the 18-pounder field guns round Nebi Samwil at the tomb of the Prophet Samuel, where the 52nd and 75th Divisions were having a bloody struggle for the crests of the Judean ridges north of Jerusalem. Besides having a shell two pounds heavier than the 18-pounder, from the very construction of the equipment the mountain guns could be carried practically anywhere a man could climb, and as howitzers could squat behind any hill. They were most powerful reinforcements in the fight, which subsequent reports showed was much helped by them. They gained a good name both for power and accuracy; also they were able to dispense with roads, and were in consequence popular with the Australians, who later on were working in the country east of Jordan.

Oswald had another reason for pleasure in seeing these weapons used on a battle front. In 1909, when first he went on the Artillery Committee, these howitzers existed on paper, and one had been made as an experiment. In its shooting trials it showed exceptional accuracy for a howitzer, and its range of 6000 yards was lengthy and reliable for so small a weapon. It was in two parts, which locked together with a quarter turn of a screw. All its equipment was experimental and fairly satisfactory, but its carriage was heavy and yet

somewhat light for its work. Oswald was prepared to accept this unsatisfactory carriage for
the reasons that have been set forth previously
as regards the immediate acceptance of the 2.75
mountain gun—that once a gun is in the service
its minor defects will be eliminated by those
who have to use it, provided the defects were
minor. But in the case of this 3.7-inch howitzer
the carriage could not be called a minor defect.
It was a serious one, and one which in experiment at Shoeburyness in 1911 or 1912 had a
bad failure. This failure came about rather
as a surprise. Oswald had asked that the trail
or ground end of the carriage should be rested
against rock, instead of earth, a circumstance
that happens in mountainous and other places,
and is unavoidable for a mountain gun. The
gun was fired in this position, and it happened
that the muzzle was raised—or elevated, as it
is called—to such a height that the breech was
lowered to a corresponding position. This
position by a curious chance caused an
important portion of the breech to be in line
with a projection at the back end of the trail.
The extra bit the gun recoiled or went back in
its carriage, due to being against rock and not
earth, made the breech hit the trail sufficiently
hard to seriously damage the machinery and
to make a repair necessary. This chance acci-
dent was fortunate; as Oswald said, " the luck
of the British Army to discover things in time."
It was, however, obvious that the carriage as

it stood would not do. The necessity for a series of further changes in the carriage was obvious, and the question was put to Oswald, as Associate member for Mountain Artillery on the Artillery Committee, whether it was worth while to go on with the 3.7-inch howitzer at all. Oswald strongly advised going on, as the gun portion was so accurate in its shooting powers, and as it was not to be expected that the 2.75 gun firing its 10-pounder shells was likely to remain a suitable weapon for ever.

The result was a drastic change in the make and pattern of the gun carriage, which was split down the middle. This allowed the two pieces of the trail or hind supports to be placed as separate supports, which jointly supported the gun when fired, while permitting it—the gun part—to come back safely on firing between the two pieces of the trail. A most convenient carriage resulted, which allowed fire to be brought to bear to a considerable extent to right and to left without moving the carriage round. This convenience, together with a very good shooting gun, made the 3.7-inch howitzer a weapon well in keeping with the desires of mountain artillery up to even 1920. Oswald had in consequence some reason to be pleased on that day in 1917 when he first saw the 3.7-inch howitzer going into battle near Jerusalem.

The story now returns to happenings at Bordon, where Oswald is training 60-pounder

batteries in 1916.   The battle of Jutland had
been fought.   Oswald heard the first news with
satisfaction, as it seemed to him obvious that
if the German Fleet were home again they were
beaten; if they had won they would be out.
He did not understand how the Admiralty
notification could be blamed.   Of course every
one wanted a Trafalgar, but could not have it
in the bad light.   After this came the real
blow, Kitchener's death, a terrible loss.

CHAPTER 10.

61st GROUP GOES ABROAD.

Here continues the record of the 61st Heavy Artillery Group in 1916 and part of 1917, till its arrival in Palestine in September, 1917. As commanding the Royal Garrison Artillery 60-pounder instructional camp at Bordon, Lieut.-Colonel O.C. Williamson Oswald, R.G.A., was directed in July, 1916, to form the 61st Heavy Artillery Group Headquarters for service with the Salonika Army. He had been some four months out of the line in France, as stated in Chapter 8, and had reorganized Bordon 60-pounder instructional camp to the satisfaction of the R.A. at the Horse Guards, so he was permitted to be relieved of Bordon and to take command of 61 H.A. Group Headquarters.

The group was manned mostly by men under the Lord Derby scheme, as were the 60-pounder batteries being formed at Bordon at the time. This type of man proved to be very valuable in the R.G.A. As regards the supply of officers, it was good. Of the Lieut.-Colonels and Majors at Bordon, besides temporarily unfit and regulars — such as Lieut.-Colonel Pitman, Crawford, D.S.O., and Mathews — who gradually recovered from their wounds and illness and mostly went to fight again, there were Lieut.-Colonels Cleaver and Hamersley, M.P., Major Grepe, and others, most patriotic men and energetic recruiters.   In most cases it was the policy of the Commandant to recommend that these senior officers should take out and command 60-pounder batteries, even when their scientific or physical capabilities were not up to that of the regulars.   He pointed out that many of the regular Captains and Majors R.G.A. had come to him to take up commands in a state of health not fit to go straight into the line again, that the senior officers, mostly Territorials, who had been previously put back from the active command of batteries which were going overseas, could well stand the racket of a few weeks or months in command of 60-pounder four-gun batteries in the line; that there was a tendency for too many pets of various expeditionary forces to be prematurely pushed up to battery command, leaving the junior ranks weak and depleted, that a few seniors could well go into the line until they were worn out.   This proposal was accepted, and it is understood that some very useful work was done by these seniors, while relief was afforded to the regular officers, both junior and senior.

The training at Bordon consisted of completing the training given at Winchester by Lieut.-Colonel H. W. M. Parker, R.G.A., now

unfit to serve abroad owing to wounds.   Much
night work was done, and a scheme in open
warfare with shell was carried out at Larkhill,
Salisbury   Plain,   under   Brigadier-General
Drake, whose advice and sympathy encouraged
the batteries and led to improvement.   Sometimes inspections were not so successful: remarks were taken down at the time and passed
on to the training authorities at the Horse
Guards, who peaceably and with skill arranged
to inspect the 60-pounders, to the relief of the
Commandant at Bordon.   Such matters as
an objection to the wearing of soft caps seemed
too inopportune to be of any use to young
non-regular officers badly wanted at the front.
As time passes what is essential becomes somewhat befogged, so perhaps this record of a
phase in the Army when dress was not a major
fetish may be useful.   Real smartness is
always a great asset, but no one can say that
this was endangered by the soft cap, a necessity
where luggage is nil and a steel helmet is the
fighting head-dress.   Further, at Bordon the
various Group headquarters and 60-pounder
batteries were equipped, horsed and armed up
to the scale of Army Form G 1098 for 60-
pounders.   This G. 1098 was an official list of
everything needed by the battery or other
formation during the war.   The source of
supply was from Aldershot, and the roads
through Farnham became bad from the constant traffic of lorries.   This defect in the

ordinary wear of an English macadam road surface is due to the drive of the mechanical wheel with solid rubber tyres. The road becomes roughened across its surface at right angles to its direction in waves of from one to even six inches in height and depth. Each lorry by its drive exaggerates the height and depth of the lateral waves, until the road becomes impassable, and even before this state is reached the road is very uncomfortable to traverse. In France the roads that resist this action are the pavé roads with stone blocks, so long as no stone is loosened.

In the summer of 1916, the King and Queen were in Aldershot, and Lt.-Colonel Williamson Oswald was warned that he must let his moustaches grow at the corners, since shaving the upper lip so as to shorten the moustache was anathema at Court, as it savoured of a Charlie Chaplin look. Much astonished, he grew the requisite corner of bristle, but H.M. came not near Bordon, and in a moment of absent-mindedness the requisite bristle disappeared on the razor. That day the King and Queen graciously visited the R.G.A. at Bordon. No need to say that both were charming. They were escorted round the great lines of the 60-pounder guns which were drawn up in imposing display, and moved off for exercise and training as the King and Queen finished their inspection battery by battery. Eight batteries were present, as far as can be remembered.

One young Battery Commander, Captain Wooll-combe, wearing the ribbon of the Military Cross, was asked if he had got his decoration, and, as he was going to the front with his battery within the week, the King particularly asked that he should be present at the next weekly investiture of honours. This was arranged for by Colonel Williamson Oswald with the Court officials on the spot; in spite of their righteous horror of such an irregularity, however, Oswald pointed out it was the King's own invitation and must be arranged for. The King knows a lot about heavy horses; he was also interested in the R.G.A., as some of his own servants had joined this part of the Army. The Queen asked about India, and also whether Mesopotamia could be manned by Indian soldiers alone, on account of the climate. Oswald said that the Indian soldiers were second to none, but for some reason they always seemed to do best with a stiffening of British. Both their Majesties speak very pure English, such as is spoken by English officers both in the pre-war Army and Navy. There was no accent and no pinching of the vowels like one hears sometimes in the Church, or as Kipling says in the Pundit (Schoolmaster) class. Mrs Williamson Oswald and her three young daughters—Praxeda, Ingleby and Alethea—were present, and their loyal greetings received a specially gracious bow from their Majesties.

Equipped, then, by the 8th August, 1916, the

61 Heavy Artillery Group left Avonmouth, or some such harbour, and embarked on the "Minewaska." On board were the personnel of four siege batteries, 6 inch Howitzer, of 26 cwt., under Major Nuttall, R.G.A. The Peerless lorries and four-wheel-drive lorries and Sunbeam motor cars of these batteries and of the 61st Group Headquarters were under Lyne, Harrison and others (see Note 10), and went in another ship. The voyage was un-eventful, though at the south point of Greece the destroyer of the French Navy, which should have met them, did not turn up, and the ship had to go about and retrace her course till some three or four hours later the destroyer bustled up, and the voyage was then continued through the submarine-infested islands into Salonika Harbour.

CHAPTER 11.

MACEDONIA.

WILLIAMSON OSWALD, now a Colonel, reported to Major-General Onslow, Major-General Royal Artillery, or M.G.R.A., Salonika, and met his staff, Majors Holbrooke and Garwood. The siege howitzers with Oswald were the first mobile lorry-drawn Siege guns to reach the British Salonika Force. In a few days Col. Williamson Oswald was sent on a reconnaisance along the Seres road, towards the Struma valley, with Lt. Brookhouse, R.G.A., orderly officer, and Major Luck in the group car, a Sunbeam. A position supporting the XVIth Corps was chosen, and the 60 miles of very bad road was traversed by Major Luck's battery with the four-wheel-drive lorries in under 48 hours, and their presence was decisive in stopping a Bulgar attack that developed at this period, the end of August or beginning of September, 1916, on the XVIth Corps. This XVIth Corps was very weak, mainly from malaria caught in the Struma valley.

As an example of the mobility of these 6-inch howitzer batteries, four of them did a flank march later in the year after the battle of Sep-

tember on the Vardar. From the Vardar they
marched in 48 hours nearly 80 miles in the
Struma front, first over hard natural mud roads
and then by the bad Seres road to the right
bank of the Struma, under command of Lt.-Col.
Holbrooke, who had taken over the 37th H.A.
Group and received these batteries for the time
being as his command.

After the Struma reconnaissance, in August,
1916, by Col. Williamson Oswald, the 61st H.A.
Group relieved the 37th H.A. Group, now under
Holbrooke, on the line facing the celebrated Pip
Ridge, near Kalinova. The march from
Salonika was about 40 miles, the first stage
being in a westerly direction along a well-made
road as far as the valley of the Galiki river,
then a turn north along the left bank of the
river till a crossing was made by a good bridge
about a mile north of the railway bridge on the
Salonika-Janes line, at Naresh, about 17 miles
W.N.W. of Salonika. Once the valley of the
Galiki was left behind, together with the mountainous ground round Salonika, quite a new
country stretched out as far as the hills running
east and west which rise north of Lake Ardzan
and Kilindir and Hirsova villages. This
country was a rolling plain with a few
ruined villages. The surface was hard and
apparently a light loamy soil. Over this
for twenty miles the motor car and lorry
with the few horses and one general service
waggon, which constituted the transport of the

group headquarters, all managed to make good time though the tracks were occupied by an Italian division moving in the same direction for about 10 miles of the journey. The country was very suitable for horses, and it is supposed that it is that portion of ancient Macedonia which, in about 400-300 B.C., was celebrated for horses and furnished them to Alexander the Great's army.

In 1916 and 1917 the country was practically a deserted grassy waste and a mosquito-breeding place. The weather during the march of the 61st Group, was very hot, being early September. The line had been fairly stabilised and Genl. Wilson's XIIth Corps was fighting along it. The Corps held from the Vardar left bank at Stokol up to the French, who were near the south shore of the six-mile wide circular Lake Doiran, and who were gradually handing over as far as this point. Eastwards an Italian force, of about a Division, held the Krusha Balkans from the south edge of Lake Doiran up to the British XVIth Corps, which held the Struma valley and on to the Gulf of Orfano, near Mount Athos. The position of the 37th Group Headquarters, now taken by the 61st, was only a temporary one, in a cleft in the ground, and through no fault of the group it was all flies, heat, and dust, and difficult of approach with a severe climb to a battle station, really an observing post, on a ridge which had a circumscribed view of the distant Vardar

valley.   Acting on experience in France, Col.
Williamson Oswald, as soon as circumstances
allowed, removed to a battle headquarters at
Kalinova that was more central and more
approachable from his various batteries.   The
telephone exchange first moved and was carefully dug in; later the rest moved, and at once
experienced a shelling, but, owing to the shell
being only 4.2-inch gun and the shelters being
well dug in, no trouble was incurred.   From
that onwards this headquarters proved satisfactory.   The old battle station had been taken
over by the 6-inch MK. VII. Battery, 43 Siege,
of 3 guns, of nearly 10 miles range, from Gallipoli.   It was caterpillar-tractor drawn and
commanded by Major Aubrey Thompson,
R.G.A.   During the British holding attack of
September, 1916, when the main results were
the taking of Florina by the French, the frontage of attack for the British was from the
Vardar to a point about 6 miles east of it,
marked roughly by a north-south line at the
east end of Lake Ardzan.

The heavy artillery fired for four days from
the 11th September, 1916, as follows:—37 H.A.
Group near the Vardar with 4 batteries of
6-inch howitzers, of 26 cwt., fired 100 rounds,
weighing 100 pounds each per gun per day—
total, 6400 rounds, supplied from Karasouli rail
head.   These batteries had 4-wheel-drive lorry
draught.   61 H.A. Group near Lake Ardzan
and Kalinova, with 3 batteries of 60-pounders

(horse draught), fired 100 rounds per gun per day—total, 4800 rounds supplied from Janes rail head; and 2 guns of 127 S. Battery, R.G.A., 6-inch how., of 26 cwt., with 4-wheel-drive, fired 50 rounds per gun per day—total, 400 rounds, with supply from Karasouli; as well as 3 guns of 43 Battery, R.G.A., 6-inch MK. VII. guns, which fired a total 420 rounds in all, and they were also supplied from Karasouli. The total was 12,000 rounds, taking 210 lorry loads and costing about £36,000. The object of this attack was to prevent the transfer of enemy troops from the XIIth Corps front. All batteries of heavy artillery may be taken as having 4 guns from September, 1916, to August, 1917, except 43 S.B., which had 3 guns. At this period, September, 1916, the heavy artillery was a much-puzzled force. For instance the move of Group battle-headquarters, as described above, was queried by remarks over the telephone beginning "What the ——" and ending in "Oh, all right." There was no vice in this perplexing treatment; once confidence was established nothing could have been more considerate than the treatment received from the higher R.A. people of the corps. Various causes contributed. One was the foresight of General Onslow, M.G.R.A., who, after September, 1916, provided reduced charges for the 60-pounder and 18-pounder guns of the force and suitable fuzes for their shrapnel when these charges were used.

It may be explained to a non-technical reader that for a gun only one sort of cordite ammunition is provided, so that though a howitzer can squat down in a hole and shoot its shell at various angles out of the hole by means of the selection of the power of one of its various cordite cartridges, the gun has to choose a position which suits the unchanging power of its one cordite cartridge. Now General Onslow's provision of reduced charges gave the guns two cartridges each to select from, and so turned the 60-pounders and 18-pounders into potential howitzers on an emergency, and thus greatly widened the choice of ground for gun positions. The reduced charges, which are practically half-sized cartridges, particularly helped those responsible for choosing these positions. This came to pass as regards the 60-pounder positions from one proviso which had been insisted upon by some one in high command, namely, that 60-pounder fire was always to be available for a defending and protective barrage (see explanation page 200) just in front of the Allied trenches in case of an attack by Germans and Bulgars who held this front. This order is an example of how an apparently simple order sometimes leads to many complications. With only the full-power cordite cartridge available, the above proviso required the 60-pounder guns to be placed in positions inconveniently and hazardously near the crest of the protecting ridges. This was

H

the only way to barrage just in front of the
British front trenches, which were away down
in the forward hollows. Two great disabilities
were suffered in consequence by the one weapon,
the 60-pounder, which had a reasonably long
range, up to 13,000 yards and more, that is, up
to about 7½ miles. One disability was that the
60-pounders could not utilze their long range
to its full power. If pushed far forward, so as
to get the best and longest ranges for their
shells to fall amongst the distant enemy, they
could not get into a hole for shelter as they
were still required to cover the front trenches,
and to do so they had to be posted almost, if not
quite, in the open. They had to fire practically
point blank to get their shells into the area
where the front trenches and no man's land lay.

The second disability was that, even in positions further back, the 60-pounder batteries
having to be up so high in order to cover front
trenches were close to the ridges which hid
them and were always being spotted. The 60-
pounder positions were shelled so constantly up
to September, 1916, that their annihilation was
probable. These guns have a large and vivid
flash by night and a conspicuous dust cloud by
day, combined with some smoke when fired by
day. As there were not many of these guns
available, it will be seen that their possible
annihilation was serious and possible unless,
colloquially speaking, they could get hidden in
a hole.

The widening of the choice of ground for 60-pounder positions, owing to the permission to use the reduced charges, completely got round the two above-mentioned disabilities.

With increasing confidence in the ability of the heavy artillery to hold down their job, batteries of 60-pounders on the XIIth Corps front gradually were worked into positions which gave immunity from destructive and neutralising enemy fire. The few 60-pounder batteries were able to work at full power and at long ranges. By the winter, 1916-17, they probed well into the enemy's lines, while they could employ reduced charges for front-line defence and barrage fire if required.

In February, 1917, the arrival of a son, Oswald Robert (Robin), was announced by telegram to Colonel Williamson Oswald, and there was great jubilation and many congratutions, while the Group Headquarters toasted the " new recruit."

CHAPTER 12.

THE mountainous terrain in which the XIIth Corps was acting often made the occupation of 60-pounder gun positions very difficult. Some guns had to be lowered by tackles down slopes to their positions after an approach by night along an exposed mountain road. The domination and possession of the " Pip " ridge by the enemy gave great scope to the enemy's observation. It seems wonderful that many of the 60-pounder positions were occupied for weeks and months before discovery came. Two very useful positions, for example, on the east or right, were taken over from the French heavy 12-centimeter guns. One was fairly orthodox, being in a valley, up which it was possible to fire over the divide at the head of the valley. 181 H. Battery went in here in 1916, and was in position till the battery, under Major Justice, went to Palestine in the autumn of 1917. This position could not have filled the front trench barrage proviso above mentioned without reduced charges. Apparently the French had different methods

114

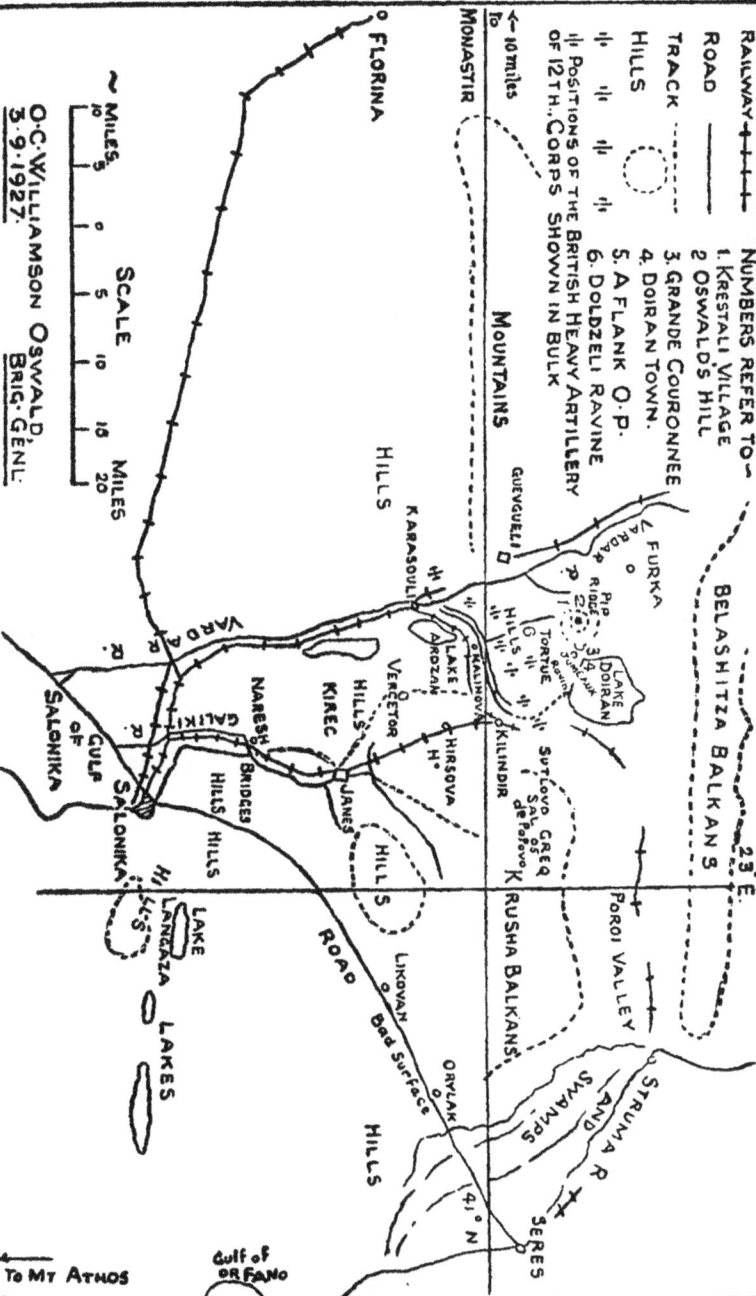

PART OF MACEDONIA · 1916-17 ·

NUMBERS REFER TO:—
1. KRESTALI VILLAGE
2. OSWALD'S HILL
3. GRANDE COURONNEE
4. DOIRAN TOWN.
5. A FLANK O.P.
6. DOLDZELI RAVINE

RAILWAY
ROAD
TRACK
HILLS

POSITIONS OF THE BRITISH HEAVY ARTILLERY
OF 12TH CORPS SHOWN IN BULK

←10 miles
to

O.C.WILLIAMSON OSWALD,
BRIG·GENL.
3·9·1927.

SCALE
MILES   10   5   0   5   10   15   20   MILES

of defending their front-line trenches.   Similarly the other position required reduced charges.   This was a most remarkable place. Both Brig.-General White Thomson, B.G.R.A., newly appointed to the XIIth Corps, and Col. Williamson Oswald, were somewhat impressed by its unorthodoxy (see sketch*), but they exchanged the remark that the French have probably forgotten more about artillery than the British ever knew, so it is as well to try it. Tried it was by Major Vanderkiste, D.S.O., R.G.A. (see note 22), and 13 heavy battery 60-pounders, and became a most formidable and destructive instrument.   In rear was a cliff. Immediately in the rear of the 4 guns, and between their positions and the cliff, was a stream with about a foot depth of water, but with high banks which permitted a rise of water of 3 or 4 feet, so that the gun platforms were safe.   There was a wide arc of fire, some 45 degrees or more each way, and a sufficient clearance over the ridges in front for distant ranges.   The communication was easy, as a good track ran along the left or western flank, though to reach it the guns had to come out from the right flank of the position and in front of the muzzles of the left section.   In front of the guns were the shelters of the officers and men dug in to the cliff, which guarded them from the front.   This cliff curved away so that the left muzzles were nearest to it, but it was just far enough forward to prevent the blast of the guns from reaching the shelters. It was an unorthodox position for shelters which worked well in practice. This position was often searched for; sometimes shell on the cliff or in the stream seemed to indicate that its discovery had happened, but no, time proved that these were chance shots only. Eventually 1917 came and the departure of the 61st Group to Palestine found a 60-pounder battery still here firing on Doiran town and neighbourhood. The O.P. left by the French was equally unorthodox. It had very good observation. It consisted of a small bench quite unprotected, situated among bushes on a crest. By sitting on the bench the observer's head was among the bushes; he was partially concealed. The British retained this observation post, but dug a burrow up to the bench and defended it; while for further protection, as time went on, a tunnel was made to the far side of the crest and head-cover provided. Another position consisted of 209 Siege Battery in the Doldzeli Ravine. This was a narrow and deep ravine running south from the Pip ridge towards Kalinova. Major Tomlinson placed his 6-inch howitzers along this ravine, firing north; it was practically four single-gun positions, and his gun corrections for firing must have been most complicated. This battery survived in this position from about December, 1916, till June, 1917, when it went to Palestine. The length of ravine the battery occupied was well over 400 yards, and the line of firing of the rear gun went roughly over all the other three.

Major W. F. F. Scott, M.C., had a battery, 205 Siege, in the most forward position occupied by the 6-inch Siege Batteries. His guns were cut into a forward slope with a cliff in front. The ravine they were in was narrow in rear and their flashes were exposed from reflection on the banks behind. This battery suffered most from gas, and after the May battle, 1917, the position became untenable and had to be abandoned. 205 Siege Battery received 1000 enemy shell between 13th April, 1917, and 13th May, 1917. Gas shell fired on them lowered their rate of fire approximately 50 per cent., but under the ordinary shell fire there was no slackening. It may be noted that some recommendations for gallantry are recorded in the war diary of 61 H.A.G. for May, 1917, which concern these events. It was not till after May 23rd, 1917, that, the enemy fire having increased, the battery was moved. Their casualties, taking one example at one gun, occurred when some of a detachment were wounded, and in the effort to clear them the gas masks of some of the detachment came off and these men were gassed. Near here two chargers with Toon, a groom, also were gassed. The history of these horses was followed up, and one of them, Tommy, never was good for a gallop again, whilst the other, Fan, became a " flesh abrasion " casualty, so the effect of gas is not known. This battery of Major Scott's was very crowded.

Originally the position was selected for two guns, and only from necessity for fire in the battle were four guns put there. The forcing of four guns into the place did not succeed, though the frontage was sufficient; the cumulative flash and smoke of four guns gave the position away after a day or two, and although two guns might have survived and done useful work four were ultimately rendered practically useless. This is given as an example of loss of power owing to gun crowding. Such guncrowding may be justified for a short operation, but its disadvantages must be accepted in a prolonged struggle. In siting heavy guns, therefore, the question, whether a short or prolonged struggle is anticipated, is a matter of importance and may be a dominating factor.

The struggle in Macedonia from September, 1916, to August, 1917, during the period 61 Heavy Artillery Group was there, was an uphill matter both physically and morally, especially as regarding the task set the British, in which the heavy artillery shared. The main efforts took place in the Monastir direction, while the British efforts included very active heavy artillery action on the Doiran front, where the XIIth Corps possessed most of the heavy artillery of the British Force. The enemy had several 8-inch howitzer batteries and some long-range 15-cm. or 5.9-inch guns with a stream-line shaped shell which had a pointed apex. This apex was of thin steel and covered the fuse and

the normal head of the 15-cm. shell, thus giving
ranges of over 20,000 yards, over 11 miles.   The
enemy were well supplied with smaller natures
of guns, and were said to have a proportion of
German and Austrian artillery among the
Bulgars, while it was reported that a strong
German division occupied the left bank of the
Vardar river opposite Guevgueli.

Commencing from the east of Lake Doiran,
where for 28 miles the Poroi valley slopes
towards the Struma, the ground is low and flat.
To the south of this valley are the Krusha
Balkans which dominate the Poroi valley from
the south, containing some very pleasant
country, and were able to be held safely by the
Allies: first, in August, 1916, the Italians, while
ultimately in the winter of 1916-17 the British
of the XIIth Corps took over the western part
of the Krusha Balkans.   To the north of the
Poroi valley, which lies between Lake Doiran
and the R. Struma valley, there rise very
abruptly the Beles or Belashitsa Balkan.   These
mountains, tipped with snow from about November, 1916, to April, 1917, formed a formidable
wall to the north.   An offshoot round the west
end of Lake Doiran with a dominating spur
called the Dub, or the P. (or "Pip") ridge,
stood west of Doiran town, of which the highest
point was "Pip One," height 1793 feet, or 537
metres, and a lesser spur between Doiran town
and the Dub, about three-quarters of the height
of the latter, called the Grande Couronnée.   To

the west of the Pip ridge the wall of the Beles
range receded, and where the mountains
crossed the line of the Vardar river at
Guevgueli there was a lowering of the mountain
wall.   A German division, as before mentioned,
was reported to occupy the key of this gap,
which stretched from the Vardar river on the
west to the spurs of the Pip ridge at Krastali.
This gap was about 8 miles across from west
to east, and in it the main features were low
hills of under 100 feet in height and of gentle
slopes.   These hills helped the German-Bulgar
defence almost as well as the more formidable
wall to the east, and for this reason the XIIth
Corps, stretching from the Vardar to near
Kilindir, and the south-east of Lake Doiran was
obliged to hold a curved front of some miles in
excess of the 18 miles in a direct line.   This
front was held by three divisions—the 60th,
22nd, and 26th—during the time 61 H.A. Group
was in Macedonia.   The 60th Division came
into the line in late 1916.   Owing to the great
frontage of the Corps and the capacity of
defence of the gap held by the Germans, no
serious attack was pushed on the Guevgueli to
Pip ridge gap against the enemy after the holding attack of September, 1916.   Between then
and the attacks of April, 1917, and May, 1917,
the heavy artillery was gradually reinforced,
and its activity was considerable.   The policy
decided upon was great heavy artillery support;
consequently the infantry, who were weak in

rifle strength, were encouraged to call for heavy
artillery support on any reasonable pretext.
This support was given in the nature either of
intense fire, if enemy infantry movements were
suspected or of neutralising (see explanation
page 199) fire on the enemy field artillery and
suspected enemy positions.   Other reasons for
British fire were retaliation, where enemy field
guns and howitzers firing on the British
infantry were causing annoyance and loss, or
counter-battery (see explanation page 199)
destructive work on all natures of enemy guns.
At this time the maps were entirely composed
from air photographs, and it required long
study to realize the features of the ground.
Separate " Flash-spotting " and " Sound-ranging " units did not exist in those days.   Flash
spotting from O.P.'s had to be carried out with
great diligence and resulted in discovery of
many hostile positions.   One group of guns,
however, defied detection even up to the taking
of Pip 4½ by the 22nd Division in April, 1917.
The forward trench here was made by the
Pioneers of the South Wales Borderers, who
suffered much loss, but Major Fairtlough,
R.F.A., who had a battery of 60-pounders, discovered this group of guns, whose position was
hidden by two knolls hardly distinguishable in
in the air map.   This discovery led to the
neutralisation of the enemy guns behind one hill,
which in consequence was called Oswald's hill,
as a measure of thanks to the Corps Heavy

Artillery for their relief, and this neutralisation
led to a more peaceful time for the new forward
trenches at Pip 4½.

Other enemy guns which defied detection, or
which were able to shift position and again open
fire, were some 8-inch howitzers, believed to be
Austrian ships' guns, which were hidden by the
main massive of the Grande Couronnée. These
howitzers, firing 200-pound shells, used to fire
at what appeared their extreme ranges, but
they could not reach much more than two miles
inside the British front line on the Lake Doiran
to Pip ridge sector. They fired pointed armour-
piercing shell with base fuze, and had many
"duds" at these extreme ranges. They were
consequently obviously not for offence, but in
the British holding attack of April, 1917, their
real obect was discovered, as these 8-inch batteries formed a hostile barrage along the bed
of the Jumeaux ravine, which divided the
Tortue hill from the Grande Couronnée, and ran
between the two armies. Here in the confined
and rocky space the shells fired were well within
effective range, were very accurate, and deton-
ated with power. These detonations, for instance, laid out some sections of Colonel Rocke's
Wiltshire Battalion of the 26th Division, who
were found lying as though asleep, having been
many of them destroyed without wound.

The main British crossing of the Jumeaux
ravine was by night. It is not thought that a
crossing by day would have given more chance

to the British airmen to discover these guns, for
the reason that to see them it was necessary to
fly very high over the Pip ridge and the Grande
Couronnée and well into the area behind these
two heights, which were well armed with
numerous anti-aircraft guns.   This area had
been constantly searched by aeroplane previously, but so far as the 8-inch enemy howitzers
were concerned their discovery and consequent
destruction or neutralisation had not been
achieved.   Some of the positions of the 8-inch
enemy howitzers, indeed, were out of range for
any but the British 6-inch MK. VII. guns, and
of the others the majority could not be effectively reached except by 60-pounder shell, but
it may be noted that where a daylight attack
makes an enemy disclose his heavy artillery
defensive barrage to reconnoitring aircraft, a
night attack loses reason except for the first
waves of the assault, which of course get the
benefit of the darkness.

An example of a minor heavy artillery
operation during the winter of 1916-1917 may
be given as follows:—138 siege battery R.G.A.
6-inch howitzers of 26 cwt., with four-wheeled
draught, fired from 3rd to 8th December, 1916,
800 rounds of 100 lb. shell with the object of
destroying new enemy works in the village of
Krastali, at the south-west corner of the Pip
ridge massive, in order to prevent this village
from being prepared for defence as an enemy
outwork.   It is thought that the desired effect

was produced, as Krastali did not become a strong outwork.

Another example of a minor operation on the night of 23/24th March, 1917, may be given, when 37 heavy artillery group fired from twelve 60-pounder guns 295 H.E. and 89 shrapnel; from 12 6-inch howitzers 125 high explosive; and from two 6-inch MK. VII. 38 H.E.—a total of 547 shell weighing over 17½ tons and costing, say, about £1600. This expenditure probably saved the lives of many infantry soldiers engaged in the operation.

The air offensive of the Germans on the Salonika front connects this front closely with London, because it was at Salonika that the Air Squadron of high-powered machines, under a leader called Boelcke (?), appeared on the 1st February, 1917. About 2 p.m. the Germans came over the Pip ridge and for twenty minutes smashed up the XII. Corps Headquarters at Janes, devoting much bombing to the air force camp and aerodrome and to the lorry transport, which all suffered severely. They kept away from the hospitals, but searched for the ordnance dumps and damaged the station. These air machines made a new sound which was afterwards the sign of large engines like the modern heavy machines of large size. They were high up and had to remain high up, as the British anti-aircraft guns were active and dangerous. The bomb craters were shallow in most cases. It is thought the bombs had about

10 pounds of high explosive or less; the lateral spread of the pieces was along the ground, keeping only 3 or 4 inches above the surface, so that men lying down were hit.   This was brought about by some kind of point to the bomb, which caused it to burst before the body of explosive touched the ground.   The pieces into which the bombs broke up were very small, some collected were not more than quarter-inch cubes.   The shallowest trenches or ditches gave immunity, so that when Colonel Williamson Oswald encountered these same German air bombs in London in the summer of 1917, while he was on leave, he was able to arrange that his family should take refuge in a slightly underground kitchen in their Hampstead house, the floor of which was about three feet below the street level.   However, after a bit, Mrs Oswald moved, as she found the children upset, one child (Ingleby) creeping wisely under the table, while Alethea, aged 4, exclaimed: " Here is another dam air raid!"

To return to Janes on 1st February, 1917, there was 190 H.B., a new battery of 60-pounders at Janes, under Captain Fairtlough, R.F.A., which was being inspected at watering by Colonel Williamson Oswald when the first big air attack came over.   The men and horses had to stop all movement for the twenty minutes of the raid.   Only one man showed signs of nervousness by trying to approach a ditch, and this only through a misunderstand-

J

ing.   This steadiness of a new battery was very
creditable.

These German machines dominated the
British and allied air forces for some weeks,
wrecking much of the Salonika base and
causing great casualties there on their first
attack on it, but the allied machines attacked
them on their return journey from Salonika,
though the allies were much weaker.   There
were many reports about this German air
detachment, that they had a *train de luxe* for
themselves and their planes and stayed in no
one place; later, that having had sufficient
experience on the weak Salonika front, they
went off in their *train de luxe* to bomb London
from the Western side of Europe.

CHAPTER 13.

DURING the winter of 1916 to 1917 the strength of the heavy artillery of the XIIth Corps increased from two group headquarters, 37 and 61, with their necessary batteries, to two more groups, namely, 82 H.A. Group under Lt.-Col. H. B. Mayne, in the early spring, and 75 H.A. Group, Lt.-Col. Macdonald, on 26th May, 1917. In consequence of the increase the B.G.R.A., White-Thomson of the XIIth Corps, reorganized the heavy artillery of the Corps. 61 Heavy Artillery Group became Headquarters XIIth Corps Heavy Artillery on the 13th March, 1917, with Colonel O. C. Williamson Oswald as Corps Heavy Artillery Commander, and with command over 37th H.A.G., Lt.-Col. Holbrooke; 82 H.A.G., Lt.-Col. Mayne; and subsequently 75 H.A.G., Lt.-Col. Macdonald, an officer also well known as the author of some celebrated regimental records. The existent heavy artillery organization of groups allowed this arrangement, as it was then feasible to detach the batteries which were under 61 H.A. group headquarters, and to give these batteries to the

other two group headquarters, namely, 37 and
82. With a brigade organization this reorgani-
zation would not have been so simple, as batteries are an integral part of an artillery
brigade. The question of pay for Colonel
Williamson Oswald did not arise, as he was on
Indian rates of pay. He was most loyally
supported by his group headquarter's officers
and men and by Major A. J. Thompson acting
as Brigade Major and detached from 43 Siege
Battery for the purpose. The adjutant, Capt.
W. Matthews, loyally took over Staff-Captain's
duties, and Lt. J. Brookhouse, orderly officer,
acted in the responsible position of Counter
Battery (see explanation page 199) Staff
Officer.

The 61st Group Headquarters had moved
from Kalinova to Hirsova, near Kilindir, in the
winter of 1916, when the French left Kilindir,
and they now went to a more central position
at Vergetor, about 5 miles N.W. from Janes
12th Corps headquarters. From that date this
organization lasted till 61 Group left the
Salonika front on 17th September, 1917, sailing
for Alexandria, where it arrived on 21st
September, 1917 (see note 12).

Bearing this organization in mind, the story
of the heavy artillery duties on the XIIth Corps
front resolve themselves into trench warfare
and the battles of April and May, 1917. The
British XIIth Corps had a hard task, continually
pounding against a very strong position: trying

to find a weak place and so keeping up the strain
(see note 7) on the German-Bulgar force, who
had to be really strong at this point for fear
that the British might make good an offensive
and so endanger all the Bulgarians to the west
of the Vardar.   The winter was free from
malaria, but very trying because of ice, mud
and snow.   With March and April came good
fighting weather; but May was hot and the
mosquito began to attack in spite of canalisation
measures and the unpleasant anti-mosquito
ointment, with which necks, chests and cheeks
had to be smeared for all night work.   It was
truly a campaign requiring cheerfulness and
endurance.   During the winter after the col-
lapse of Roumania there was always a threat
of a sudden retreat if Mackensen or his kind
should determine on an offensive.   This and
weakness of rifle strength gave the heavy artillery much to do in the way of activity of fire
at all hours.

Offensive activity by the British increased
as the spring weather of 1917 came on.   For
the battle of April 24th and subsequent dates
the 26th Division was to attack or hold from
Lake Doiran to the Jumeaux Ravine inclusive;
the 22nd Division similarly to attack up to Pip
5 inclusive; the 60th Division held the rest of
the front up to the Vardar river.   The XIIth
Corps Heavy Artillery plan was as follows:—
For eight days' firing, 37 H.A. Group Headquarters, at Hirsova, Lt.-Col. Holbrooke was

right Counter-Battery Group and 82 H.A. Group at Kalinova, Lt.-Col. H. B. Mayne, R.G.A., was left Counter-Battery Group in addition to their other work.

37 H.A. Group Headquarters at Hirsova, Lt.-Col. Holbrooke, were detailed to fire (see note 22).

13 Heavy Battery 60 prs.—Major Vanderskiste	3 guns
196 Heavy Battery 60 prs.—Major Cobbe or Clayton	3 „
181 Heavy Battery 60 prs.—Major Justice	4 „

100 rounds per gun per day, or 8000 rounds for eight days.

134 Siege Battery 6-in. hows., 24 cwt.—Major O. Price	4 guns
138 Siege Battery 6-in. hows., 24 cwt.—Major Nuttall	4 „
205 Siege Battery 6-in. hows., 24 cwt.—Major W. F. F. Scott, M.C.	4 „

were given 150 rounds per gun per day, or 14,000 rounds for eight days.

43 Siege Battery 6-in. MK., VII.—Lt. Woodall	1 gun

had 100 rounds per day, or 800 rounds for eight days.

In 82 H.A. Group, Lt.-Col. Mayne, the distribution of ammunition for the eight days was H.E. and shrapnel, 2410 for

18 Heavy Battery 60 prs.—Major
    Gooch ... ... 4 guns
190 Heavy Battery 60 prs.—Major
    Fairtlough, M.C. ... ... 4 „
185 Heavy Battery 60 prs.—Major
    Cobbe or Clayton... ... ... 4 „
3000 rounds high explosive for the 6-inch hows.,
24 cwt., of
209 Siege Battery—Major Tomlinson... 4 guns
130 Siege Battery—Major Johnson,
    D.S.O. ... ... 4 „
For 43 Siege Battery, two 6-in. MK. VII. guns—
Capt. H. A. Shaw.
H.E. 260 and shrapnel 20... ... ... 2 guns
For artillery observation 12 aeroplanes and 2
kite balloons were provided, one kite balloon was
near water at Kalinova and was shot down by
a plane when Major Johnson was observing, and
one kite balloon was near water west of Hirsova. The neighbourhood of water was necessary to make hydrogen gas for the balloons.
The 'planes were much handicapped by the guns
firing from the high hills called the " Dub " or
the " Pips " and adjacent high ground; while
the balloons could not rise high enough to look
well over these hills.

The recorded enemy guns were on the
Doiran to Jumeaux Ravine frontage 14 barrage
battery positions, and to the west of this frontage, for which 82 H.A.G. was responsible, there
were 13 enemy barrage battery positions and 9

heavy gun positions. Fifteen enemy heavy gun positions in all are recorded on the whole of the XIIth Corps front, of which seven enemy were to be destroyed or made to move to worse positions, if possible prior to the operation. The located enemy observation posts were 22 on the front Doiran or Jumeaux ravine, and these were increased to a total of 29 enemy by 37 Group's observations; while on 82 H.A.G. front were recorded seven enemy O.P.'s increased by the Group's observations to twelve.

The battle culminated in an attack on the " Pip " ridge on the night 24/25 April, 1917, and was moderately successful in that the 22nd Division got a new line on the heights of the Pip ridge between Pips 4 and 5, which gave an improved position. In daylight on the evening of 28th April, 1917, a furious enemy bombardment began on the new British trenches from Pip 4½ to Hill 380. The two heavy artillery groups 37 and 82 were very prompt in dealing with the enemy bombardment. On this occasion the point chosen by the enemy for his counter-attack and bombardment was high up the hill of the Pip ridge and more visible to those at Corps Heavy Artillery Headquarters at Vergetor than to points nearer the front. The first bursts of enemy shell caused a quick realisation of the situation, and a precautionary defensive heavy artillery barrage was ordered and put down in front of Pip 4½, so somewhat anticipating the S.O.S. from that locality; this

barrage destroyed a large Bulgarian infantry
counter-attack at this point; reports said that
the attacking column was over a battalion, but
this has not been checked. From that time
Pip 4½ was consolidated by the 22nd Division.
The French and Allied operation towards
Monastir, of which the operation of April on
the XIIth Corps front was originally a portion,
did not materialise until May, but from the view
of minor strategy, it may be recorded that the
British operation in April appears successful,
as it seems to have led to a further increase of
the enemy forces near the XIIth Corps.   For
instance, the British heavy artillery pressure
was kept up, and culminated in a two days'
bombardment for the Doiran battle in May,
1917.   By this time the record of enemy positions shows a large increase of gun strength
opposing the XIIth Corps which was strategically advantageous to the allies.   Heavy gun
positions have increased from 15 to 25 enemy,
of which the western positions have decreased
by two; but on the Lake Doiran to Jumeaux
ravine front there are 18 heavy gun positions,
an increase of at least 12, or 200 per cent.
Field and 4.2-inch howitzer gun positions have
increased from 14 enemy on the Doiran to
Jumeaux ravine front to 36, remaining stationary on the western positions in front of 82 H.A.
Group, where 14 enemy replace the previous 13
positions.   The enemy also first used gas shell
on the 23rd April, 1917, which must have

created an extra strain on their ammunition resources. All this must have meant a weakening on some other front, probably the French at Monastir, and consequently contributed to future success.

For the May battle the XIIth Corps Heavy Artillery allotted for six days' firing:—

To 37 H.A. Group for—

60-pounders, 14 guns, 100 rounds per day, total, 8400;

6-inch howitzers, 11 guns, 150 rounds per day, total 9900;

6-inch MK. VII., 1 gun, 100 rounds per gun per day, total 600;

and to 82 H.A. Group for—

60-pounders, 12 guns, 100 rounds per gun per day, total 7200;

6-inch howitzers, 10 guns, 150 rounds per gun per day, total 9000;

6-inch MK. VII., 2 guns, 100 rounds per gun per day, total 1200;

total 60-pounders, 15,600 rounds; 6-inch howitzers, 18,900 rounds; and 6-inch MK. VII., 1800 rounds, a weight of some 1600 tons, of which over 1400 tons of steel reach the hostile area in those six days at a cost of over £110,000, if about £3 is taken as the average cost of each of these 36,000 rounds of steel shell.

After all, this was but a minor operation involving a British Army Corps making a holding attack on its normal frontage, in order to divert the enemy from detaching troops and guns to another portion of the allied line; a very necessary operation, but it cannot be considered cheap, and the above £110,000 can be considered as one item of the costs alone, costs which include all items of war-like stores, besides a cost of life running into four figures for the Corps.   Another war on the colossal scale of 1914 to 1919 may be far distant, but minor wars may be approaching; and the costings are such as to cause any but very rich or very fanatical powers or agitators to enter therein only if no other settlement is possible.   Unfortunately, it is not true that it takes two to make a quarrel. One mad dog can disturb a parish and has to be downed, regardless of cost.   The May operations on the XIIth Corps front synchronised with Sarrail's main French and Servian attack farther away to the West.   It had the desired effect, for it drew guns and perhaps forces from the enemy in front of the French and Servians.

After May, 1917, the heavy artillery work lessened, and most of the units were taken out of the line and put to drill and training in the rolling downs near Kirec, south-east of Lake Ardzan.   This was an uncomfortable period, as the fly and mosquito season was on, and the men were in tents and hankered after their shelters and dug-outs.   However, the time was well spent, and the move of certain units to the important Palestine front was foreshadowed.

The summer saw the end of 61 Heavy Artillery Group Headquarters as a super-group in Macedonia acting as Corps Artillery Headquarters. It moved to Salonika, being specially selected, as the order ran. On 17th September, 1917, it embarked, and, after a risky voyage, disembarked at Alexandria on the 21st September, 1917.

PALESTINE
A·D·1917-1918

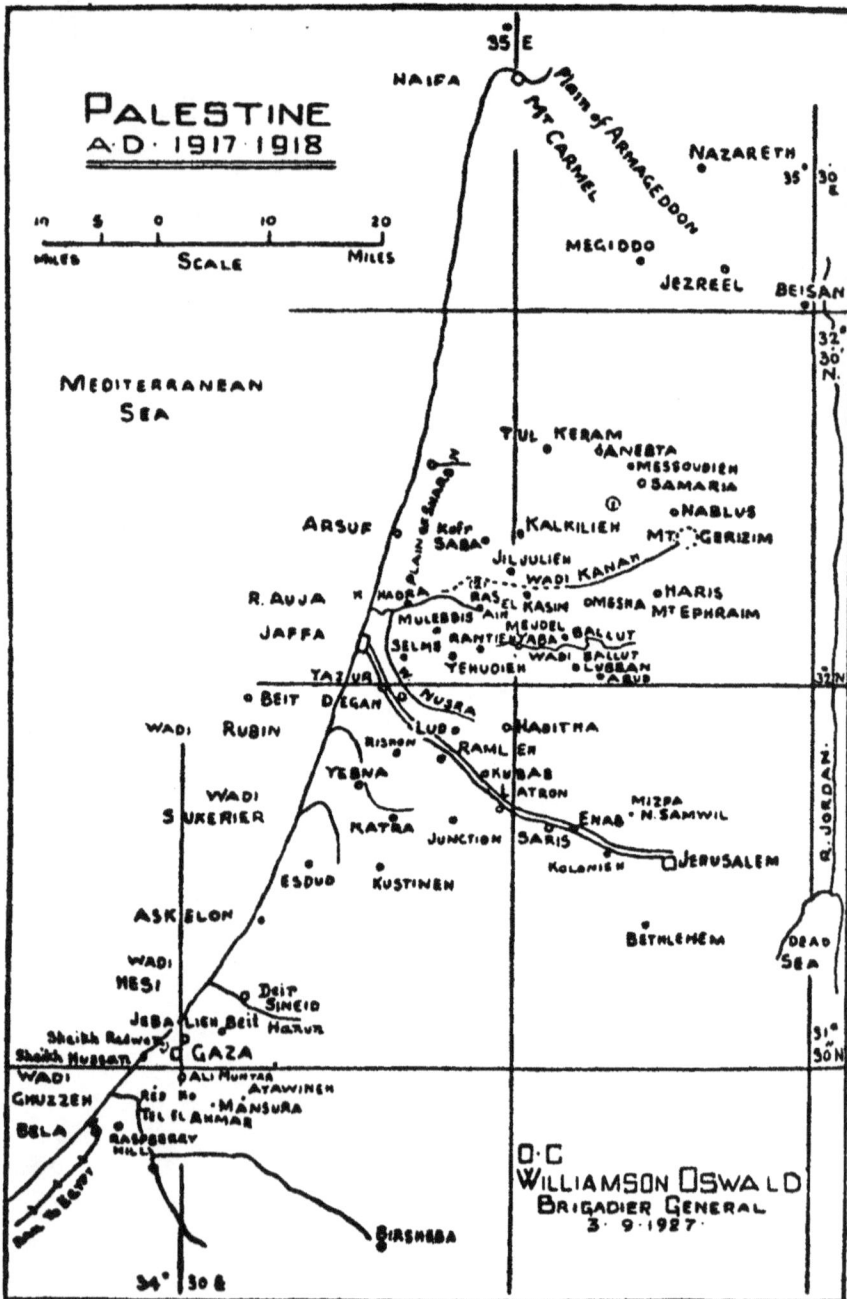

MEDITERRANEAN
SEA

O·C
WILLIAMSON OSWALD
BRIGADIER GENERAL
3·9·1927·

CHAPTER 14.

GENERALLY speaking, General Allenby, having behind him a railway line and a line of piped drinking water from Egypt, struck at the German-Turkish Army, who opposed him, in October, 1917, from Beersheba to Gaza. He out-manœuvred the enemy at Beersheba and blew a hole through their defences at Gaza, where Colonel Oswald had the good fortune to command the heavy artillery. These operations gave Allenby a line north of Jaffa (Joppa) to Jerusalem.

In September, 1918, Allenby out-manœuvred the enemy east of Jerusalem and blew a hole with his XXIst Corps and their heavy artillery, with whom Brigadier-General Oswald again was lucky enough to be working, through the Turks at Arsuf to Jiljulieh (Gilgal) on the shore of the Mediterranean Sea. Through this hole Allenby passed a whole Army Corps of Cavalry which, by getting behind the Turks via Megiddo, Nazareth and Damascus, captured their whole Army; and began the debacle of the German and Allied powers—a debacle which brought

down first Bulgaria, then Turkey, and then
Austria, thus leaving Germany alone.

27th October, 1917.   This day, the Third
Battle of Gaza began with the heavy artillery
bombardment.   There was very heavy rain
at 21.00 hours.   The nullahs and wadis were
swamped with water in the area where the
XXIst Corps heavy artillery batteries and
ammunition dumps were located.   Owing to the
sound construction of the ammunition shelters
no damage was suffered by them, and the
bombardment was not interfered with.

The organization of heavy artillery at this
time was not by brigades but by batteries.
Lieutenant-Colonels' commands were called
heavy artillery group headquarters.   These
group headquarters had a variable number of
batteries posted to them.   This method continued until some date in 1918.   After that the
Lieutenant-Colonel's command became a heavy
artillery brigade, and a certain number of
batteries became permanently, or semi-perma-
nently, part of his brigade.   In consequence of
the prevalence of the group system until 1918,
it will appear that the batteries shown in
the Corps Artillery of both XXth and
XXIst Corps were not always acting with the
Brigade R.G.A. to which they are credited.

There was no Commander Heavy Artil-
lery in the Force or in the XXIst or
XXth Corps until the 12th December, 1917.
In the XXIst Corps before this date the 61st

Heavy Artillery Group Headquarters, under
Colonel O. C. Williamson Oswald, C.B., under-
took the Brigadier's and Staff duties, and this
group should be shown in the order of Battle
of XXIst Corps till December, 1917. It had no
batteries under it for discipline at that time.
The other groups worked under its orders.
The bombardment tables were compiled by
Lieut.-Colonel Kirkpatrick, D.S.O., 97th Heavy
Artillery Group, while Lieut.-Colonel Moore,
D.S.O., 100th Heavy Artillery Group, and Lieut-
Colonel Reade, 102nd Heavy Artillery Group,
were in command on the left (west) and right
(east) counter-battery groups, with Captain
Armitage, R.F.A., as counter-battery* staff
officer. The whole of the heavy artillery in the
corps was available for neutralization* of the
enemy's guns; this during any British assault
was ruled to be their main duty.   In the
bombardment, all natures of guns took part at
various times, including the three 8-inch
howitzer batteries. The 8-inch howitzers were
of the new pattern.

The heavy artillery on the Palestine front
comprised:—60-pounders, 6-inch howitzers of
26 cwt., 8-inch howitzers, and 6-inch MK. VII.
guns, from this date till operations ceased.
Batteries had four guns.

From 27th to 31st October, 1917, the XXIst
Corps Heavy Artillery fired 13,756 rounds from
68 guns. (See note 15).

*See explanation page 199.

x

The S.O.S.* arrangements in the XXIst Corps Heavy Artillery for the Third Battle of Gaza were:—60-pounders and 6-inch howitzers, one round per gun per minute; 8-inch howitzers, one round per gun per two minutes. After five minutes one round per battery, four guns, per two minutes; and batteries to ask for further orders.

The map from G.S. 54th Division, November, 1917, Sheets A.B.C., scale 1/10,000 on white paper (see Note 8), gives the names of the enemy trenches, as devised by the British Staff. It appears to be the only copy extant, and it is important to gain and preserve copies of it for the artillery story. The reason that this map was published was that, up to late in September, 1917, all enemy trenches were known by map co-ordinates; this system was considered by the heavy artillery to be too clumsy, especially for liaison with attacking infantry, consequently the trenches were given names to each distinct length. The infantry rehearsed their attacks over full scale diagrams laid on the ground and showing the trenches as in the map. The success of this method of identification was proved, as is explained later, on November 2nd.

As recorded on the 22nd October, 1917, the located enemy battery positions on the XXIst Corps front were:—

64 positions occupied by 77-mm. guns.

---

*See explanation page 199.

12 positions occupied by 5.9-inch (15-cm.) howitzers.

6 positions occupied by 4.2-inch (100-mm.) howitzers.

2 positions occupied by two 4.2-inch (100-mm.) guns.

On the 31st October, 1917, three positions more were located, and also six naval guns, as well as the Austrian artillery headquarters.

In all, these locations comprised 87 batteries of various strengths and the six naval guns.

To continue the counter-battery records, the enemy battery positions on the 1st and 2nd November, 1917, from the sea to Ali Muntar were 37. Their artillery activity during the British infantry attack on the 1st and 2nd November, 1917, appeared to diminish*, as the neutralizing British counter-batteries increased their rate of fire. The enemy battery positions from the sea to Ali Muntar on the 4th November, 1917, had become reduced to 20, and from 16.00 hours to 17.00 hours their guns were very active. On the 6th November, 1917, the enemy positions in this area were only 18, and from 15.30 hours till 17.00 hours their guns were very active. The enemy's gun activity on the 4th and 6th seems to have been merely firing away of ammunition before a night retirement.

On the 29th, 30th and 31st October, 1917, special (lethal gas) shells were fired. The amount fired by the XXIst Corps heavy artillery

*Note 24.

was " V.N." 480 rounds, and " P.S." 180 rounds
from 60-pounders. The hours were 6 p.m. to
7.56 p.m. in five eleven-minute bursts. The
times chosen were decided on as giving the gas
the best chance in the heated climate of Palestine at that season. There was no hesitation
about using gas shell, as the enemy were allied
to the original gas-using Germans and contained German units.

Up to the end of the third battle of Gaza
the XXIst Corps heavy artillery consisted of
left and right counter-battery groups, 100 and
102, each of four 60-pounders, four 8-inch
howitzers, eight 6-inch howitzers: and one bombardment group; 97th H.A. Group, eight
60-pounders, two 6-inch MK. VII. guns, twenty-
two 6-inch howitzers, and four 8-inch howitzers.
as 300 S. Battery consisted of two 8-inch and
two 6-inch howitzers: as did 201 S.B.

2nd November, 1917.—Colonel Williamson
Oswald, commanding Heavy Artillery XXIst
Corps, about 5 a.m. on 2nd November, 1917,
received news of the partial failure of the
attack of the 163rd Brigade at 3.45 a.m.
He obtained sanction, and at about 7 a.m. the
heavy artillery re-bombarded the 163rd infantry
brigade front and so helped the 163rd infantry
brigade to hold. The enemy's trenches had
been carefully named as already described and
as can be seen in map from G.S. 54th Division,
November, 1917, sheets A.B.C. as already noted.
This method—such names as " Swan," etc.—

made possible the rapid identification of the line held by the 163rd infantry brigade, and made re-bombardment safe. An advanced party of the 163rd Brigade were missing, under a major. Their experiences under this re-bombardment would be interesting. They survived and were released at the Armistice. On asking to re-bombard, as stated above, a query regarding the endurance powers of the Royal Garrison Artillery was raised. The Colonel commanding heavy artillery stated they could go on fighting, as they had water and rations. He states: " I was amused at any doubt as to their powers; some people thought they were all out and exhausted after the intense bombardment, October 27th to November 2nd, 1917, but this was not so."

As regards the repulse of counter-attacks of the enemy on this date, the most serious one occurred in the morning. At 8.57 a.m. a barrage, on the line dividing squares G. 22 and 28 (map of Gaza) from squares G. 23 and 29, was fired by the whole of the XXIst Corps heavy artillery to assist infantry holding G. trenches in square G. 21 d. and squares G. 28 a and c. This barrage line is a north and south line, which lies on the northerly slopes of the big sand hill, Sheikh Redwan, and the south end is 500 yards west (see note 8) of the north edge of Jebalieh village. This barrage was an S.O.S. (see explanation on page 199) and is described as follows by Colonel Williamson

Oswald:—An S.O.S. barrage, carefully prepared and registered with aerial observations, had been arranged for several days previous to 27th October, 1917. It was on a line 3000 yards long, lying north and south, and placed about two miles east of Sheikh Hassan, the village on the coast north-west of Gaza town; the line was placed on the sand slopes of a prominent hill, Sheikh Redwan. The whole XXIst Corps heavy artillery were detailed for this barrage.   On warning from the 162nd infantry brigade of the direction of one serious enemy counter-attack this barrage opened.   This caught the Turkish division and pretty well wiped it out, an example of successful foresight in anticipating possible counter-attacks, due largely to the late Br.-General Simpson Baikie, B.G.R.A., XXIst Corps. From the heavy artillery point of view this barrage was decisive and consolidated the British hold on Gaza.

The role of the two 6-inch MK. VII. guns of 43 Siege Battery consisted of long-range work, which should appear in their war diary, recorded by the group possibly; but their principal decisive aim was a surprise long range and continuous bombardment of railhead. This railhead bombardment should not be confused with the naval bombardment of Deir Sineid, where naval shells were found. Railhead was about 1½ miles from the bridge over the Wadi Hesi at Deir Sineid.   This railhead was not attacked before 27th October, 1917, and it was managed by pushing the two 6-inch guns forward north of Wadi Ghuzze near Tel el Ahmar with captive balloon observation from the T of Tel el Ahmar, and also with ground observation by Captain Haskew, R.G.A., from a very exposed O.P. on Mansura ridge.   The flying machines could not see these shells and the balloon under orders of Beaufoy relieved.   The balloon was destroyed by 100 mm. shrapnel from a north-easterly direction.   The observer was hit, but jumped clear and landed safely on the edge of the Wadi Ghuzze.   Unfortunately the wind caught his deflated parachute and pulled him over a 50ft. precipice with severe injuries.   He recovered (see note 9).

The naval bombardment was to some extent indirect, and was arranged between the B.G.R.A. XXIst Corps and Lieut.-Commander Hazlefoot, R.N., Laison Officer.   Marks were put up on shore and the methods employed should be obtained from the commander for record as valuable.   Back areas were the targets.

7th November, 1917.—The 97th Heavy Artillery Group re-bombarded on the 3rd and 4th November, 1917, and detailed the trenches for bombardment on the 4th and 5th November, 1917.   There was an intense bombardment on the 5th and 6th November previous to an infantry attack, expected to come off at 4 p.m. on 6th November, but ultimately ordered for 7th November at 1 a.m.

The intense bombardment was made possible as the R.G.A. had successfully pressed for permission to fill up to 1000 rounds per gun after the bombardment of 2nd November, 1917. Subsequently after the advance of the R.G.A. there was a bother about retrieving the remaining ammunition. Colonel Williamson Oswald remarked: " That is the worst of these victories. If you want to fire all your ammunition away, you want to arrange for a repulse."

The theoretical situation shows a large Turkish force partially surrounded on the Atawineh trenches and near by. These forces are supposed to have slipped away. It is doubtful if the British " pincers," Desert Corps on the north-east, and the Indian Imperial Service Cavalry at Deir Sineid on the north-west, were as close to each other as is shown in the theoretical situation. There was a final burst of enemy artillery on the 75th Division at Sheikh Abed,* which was heavy and continued for some hours, and then stopped finally. This burst of fire is important, as it times the retreat of the artillery from the Turkish position. It appears to have occurred on the 7th November, 1917, when the enemy were still bombarding Middlesex Hill,* Queen's and Lee's Hills, the Donga and Mansura Ridge for the last time.

Also on the 8th November, 1917, the 100th Heavy Artillery Group near Wadi Ghuzze, Tel

---

* All near Mansura.

el Ahmar, fired on massed infantry at W. 6 d,
map Atawineh.   There is also a record of des-
perate Turkish resistance in this area and a lack
of water for the Desert Mounted Corps at this
period.

The blowing up of the big enemy dump on
the 8th November, 1917, mentioned by Massey
in "How Jerusalem was won," was also wit-
nessed from the top of Sheikh Redwan hill by
Colonel Williamson Oswald and his acting
Brigade Major, Major Aubrey Thompson,
D.S.O., R.G.A., as related later on.   They had
taken the opportunity of the advance through
Gaza and along the coast to get forward for a
short reconnaisance.   The route they took was
from headquarters at Raspberry Hill, where
they left Captain Matthews, R.G.A., Adjutant
and Lieutenant Brookhouse, R.G.A., group
orderly officer, with Lt.-Colonel Kirkpatrick
close by.   From here they rode north-west
across the light friable soil to the mouth of the
Wadi Ghuzze, whence they made their way
along the heavy sand of the sand dunes as far
as Sheikh Hassan village, keeping pretty well
to the coast and under cover from Ali Muntar
ridge and Gaza town.   The going here was very
heavy sea-sand.

On the matter of sand it is always necessary
to distinguish the sand of the seashore, a white
pure sand in which nothing will grow, which is
found encroaching in sand hills all along the
coast line from the Palestine-Egyptian frontier

to the neighbourhood of Askelon and Ashdod
in a band averaging, say, a mile in depth from
the sea inland and which requires great effort
to cross at all seasons. The rest of the sandy
area is a light, friable soil which grows good
crops of barley especially, and with rain binds
into a surface fitted for wheeled traffic. This
light sandy soil extends from south of the
Palestine-Egyptian frontier up to about the
Wadi Hesi and inland as far as the XXIst Corps
operations extended. Further north, as far as
Mount Carmel and the Judean Hills this friable
soil alternates with black cotton soil, which is
good going in dry weather, but a swamp with
rain. As a rule the bands of black cotton soil
border the Palestine Wadis in the coastal plain,
while the plain of Armageddon is entirely
cotton soil. The existence of these belts of
alternating cotton soil and light sandy soil gave
the advancing army some difficulty as rain and
dry weather alternated. When the country was
better known it was found in some cases possible to avoid the ground rendered difficult, for
instance to avoid cotton soil in wet weather.

On the 8th November, 1917, there was no
alternative for the advancing 52nd Division, and
with it for the two attached heavy and seige
batteries, except to use the sand-dune area of
heavy sand. The caterpillars with guns managed to get along and ultimately attained the
north bank of the Wadi Hesi, after which their
difficulties were minimised until the rain of late

November, when, to anticipate events, these batteries were well to the northward on the light sandy soil of the rolling plain which lies north of the Wadi Nusra, whose cotton soil banks border the north side of the Jaffa to Ramleh main road.   Many other caterpillars, however, were out of action in the sand dunes of Gaza on the 8th November, 1917, for want of petrol, oil and grease, and it was only by great efforts that the A.S.C. staff officer, Lieut. Fair, was able to supply them during the 8th and 9th November, 1917, with fuel and to bring them back to their headquarters near Raspberry Hill with a view to further advance.   Better lines of advance had by then been discovered through Gaza town and also east of Ali Muntar, which latter route became feasible on the retirement of the Turks from the Atawineh position.

The caterpillar difficulties became obvious to Colonel Williamson Oswald on his reconnaissance on the 8th November, 1917.   After leaving Sheikh Hassan he turned inland and saw that the hill Sheikh Redwan was composed of heavy sea sand as well.   This area was an extraordinary sight from the cases of 18-pounder shrapnel and fuzes; hardly a square yard was free from them.   His party rode up the hill and, shortly after, when on the top, a huge pillar of smoke rose up from the open plain eastwards. Immediately counting the seconds, it was possible, on the arrival of the tremendous report, to estimate the distance and, with the bearing, to locate the explosion. The point was definitely fixed in the enemy area and presaged a retreat. Roughly, the place was three miles north-east of Gaza town and the time noon.

An immediate advance was probable. The country to the east was so much more promising looking from the top of Sheikh Redwan that the reconnaissance party made up their minds to avoid the coastal sand dunes of heavy sand. This was done eventually, so far as artillery caterpillars and lorries were concerned.

The party returned roughly due south through the abandoned Turkish trenches west of Gaza town, a most difficult route through a strong position partly in deep sand well revetted and partly in the lighter sandy soil, where the gigantic prickly pear hedges, some of them twenty feet thick and with trunks over a foot in diameter, as well as the olive groves, must have been a most severe obstacle to the British infantry advance.

On about the 8th November, 1917, Colonel Williamson Oswald made a tour by Ford car as far as Beit Hanun station, and simplified thereby the duties of ammunition supply to the three Army Corps during their advance. These duties were taken up on the 8th November, 1917, as noted later. On this reconnaissance he found the most difficult portion of the advance for lorries was from the British front wire north of Red House up to the entrance of Gaza town, and that the road north of Gaza town to Beit

Hanun station was wearing out.   Ultimately the best route for lorries was found to be to keep to the east of Ali Muntar, using the wire-netting roads in the deserted British position from Belah station via Raspberry Hill and onward via the neighbourhood of Mansura ridge up to the British old front line, and so out on to the plain east of the heights which reach from west of Deir Sineid to Ali Muntar.   This route avoided the congestion in Gaza town and was used until the British railhead got to Deir Sineid.

CHAPTER 15.

THIS day, the 8th November, 1917, Br.-General Simpson - Baikie, B.G.R.A., XXIst Corps, went sick, and Colonel Williamson Oswald took over his duties and was detailed by the M.G.R.A., Major-General S. C. U. Smith, to supply ammunition to the three Army Corps on the move. Also, there was needed a supply of petrol, oil and grease for the lorries, cars and caterpillars moving the ammunition forward. This was carried by road and also by sea transport to various points on the coast. The three Army Corps were XXIst, XXth and Desert Corps. Br.-General Simpson-Baikie rejoined about 18th December, 1917.

If the Order of Battle (see note 8) of the Royal Army Service Corps in the General Headquarters and in the XXth and XXIst Corps be examined, it will be seen that the large proportion of it, namely, mechanical transport, was attached to the heavy artillery: in total 11 in the XXth and 14 in the XXIst Corps, or 25 mechanical Transport Companies were an integral part

of the heavy artillery (see notes 10 and 13).
They had come overseas as part of those units;
and when, under the doctrine of the conserva-
tion of force, siege batteries were relinquished,
their units of mechanical transport disappeared
with their batteries from the force in Egypt
and Palestine. There may have been exceptions,
but the above was the general principle. However, as mechanical transport is not exclusively
fitted up for artillery transport, as are field and
horse artillery wagons and limbers, the usefulness of caterpillar tractors and of lorries is able
to be diverted to other than artillery purposes.
This mechanical transport belonging to the
Heavy Artillery was then the only transport
that made it possible for the advancing divisions of the British Egyptian Expeditionary
Force to continue their advance with the required rapidity. The Major-General Royal
Artillery of the Force retained a minimum of
this transport for ammunition supply purposes;
this included about 40 lorries and some caterpillars with details, including Raratonga (New
Zealand) detachment all under Major Hilder.

The going was very bad through the old
trench line and No Man's Land, but here the
lorries got through the sand by means of a wire-
meshed netting road.   In Palestine the going
was better and the cotton soil made a splendid
surface till the rain came, while caterpillars
were stationed at the worst sandy patches to
drag the lorries over them.   It was found harm-

ful to attempt to solidify the sand by using the branches and leaves of the abundant prickly pear hedges.   The spikes are poisonous and very sharp, so that the only road on which such a surface was tried had to be avoided even by booted men.

Though outside the theme of the action of the heavy artillery, the comparison made between the break through in the third Battle of Gaza and the break through of the cavalry at the battle of 19th September, 1918, is of interest. Besides the great handicap the Desert Mounted Corps suffered from in November, 1917, in natural obstacles, its composition was different in the two cases.   At Sharon the preponderating force was cavalry, led by cavalry leaders and with the real cavalry spirit, namely to get round an obstacle and not to be held up by forces obviously put there to act as a block.   At Sharia the tactics were more to brush away obstacles, which may be defined as mounted infantry action, namely, action by means of rifle fire.

Coast Defence.   About the 8th November, 1917, two 60-pounders of 195 H. Battery undertook Coast Defence at Belah over the netted sea area.   They   moved   to   Jaffa   on   the   2nd December, 1918, for coast defence and were relieved there by three 4.7-inch guns with R.G.A. details unfit for the heavy artillery.   These guns came from Major Rambaut's command at Alexandria.   They remained at Jaffa till the end of August, 1918, when they went into the line north of El Lubban for the battle of Sharon.

9th November, 1917.—The coastwise front by now was the most important, and the XXIst Corps advanced rapidly.   This advance was owing to the break-through of the 52nd and 54th Divisions between Gaza town and the sea into the plains of Palestine, and had been accomplished largely by the XXIst Corps Heavy Artillery action, which saved the staunch attacks of the 52nd and 54th Divisions from consisting of holding actions only, and had permitted these attacks to become decisive between 2nd November and 7th November, 1917.

During the rapid advance of the XXIst Corps, it was noted that numbers of able-bodied villagers existed in all the villages.   In Ashdod (Esdud), for example, 20 were easily counted on the 13th November, 1917.   As the Turks had enrolled all the available man-power in their forces these were probably deserters from their ranks in borrowed garments.

11th and 12th November, 1917.—The landing of R.A. ammunition and stores north of the congestion at Gaza became possible on the 11th and 12th November, 1917.   It was done on the open beach at the mouth of the Wadi al Hesi. The stores were dragged from the mouth of the wadi on hastily made wooden sleighs over the heavy sea sand by caterpillars till they reached the lighter soil at Deir Sineid; thence these stores were transported by lorry to the fighting units, and luckily the earth tracks north kept solid till it was possible to use the beach at Nahr Sukereir.   The stores were ammunition for three corps; petrol, oil and grease were also included owing to the experience of heavy artillery needs previously gained.   Lieut.-Commander Hazlefoot (R.N. Liason) arranged for this, and the R.A. were able to supply petrol to the advanced XXIst Corps Headquarters for their Ford cars at a crucial moment.   This petrol, oil and grease supply was also a vital matter and one of the causes of the smooth working of events later.   Each lorry was also supplied with some rations and spare water for issue if wanted by R.A. and other units working on ammunition duties.   They had orders to dump these supplies at the furthest point north. These dumps are noted as they occur.   Once " Q " were able to undertake all supply of rations and water beyond railhead the necessity for spare water and rations in lorries disappeared.   As regarding communications to the rear, at 4 a.m., November 12th, the only opportunity occurred for an important conversation by telephone regarding the situation and the forwarding of ammunition and stores, between Colonel Williamson Oswald at XXIst Corps advanced headquarters and Major A. Thompson, D.S.O., acting Brigade Major Heavy Artillery.   A special switch was put in at Belah signalling station to connect the Deir Sineid to Belah line with the executive line to the heavy artillery at Raspberry Hill, near the Wadi Ghuzze.

13th November, 1917.—The R.A. ammunition and petrol were brought up to a dump near El Kustine from the Wadi Hesi under Major Hilder on the 13th November, 1917.

The acting B.G. R.A. XXIst Corps was travelling in a Ford car across country and saw the 52nd Divisional Commander Hill and his C.R.A., Br.-General F. C. Massy, near Katra, on the 13th November, 1917, whence he returned to Deir Sineid. Journeys of 50 and 60 miles were made possible by using Ford cars; and the whole country occupied thus became familiar, and its possibilities for ammunition supply became very early known.

15th and 16th November, 1917.—The R.A. ammunition and stores commenced to be brought to near Junction station by roads and tracks from Wadi Hesi on the 15th November, 1917. Also the future change of sea base from Wadi Hesi mouth to Nahr Sukereir mouth was considered on the 16th November, 1917.

17th and 18th November, 1917.—Colonel Williamson Oswald moved to El Kustine on the 17th November, 1917.

19th November, 1917.—Nahr Sukereir to Junction station began to be used as a line of ammunition supply about the 19th November, 1917. The rain which fell on the 19th did not interfere with this line of supply, but at first rather consolidated the soil. A line of advance

via Yebna (ancient Jamnia or Ibelin) to Yazur
also was developed both for caterpillar tractors
and camels about the 24th November, 1927, and
continued until about the 20th December, 1917,
when Jaffa was made secure; but even after
this date Sukereir was used and gradually
emptied of ammunition by caterpillar tractor.
The going on this line, especially from Yebna
across the Nahr Rubin to Rishon Le Zion, was
very heavy through the cotton soil after the
rain, which came early in December. By that
date supplies of ammunition at Junction,
Ramleh and Yazur were sufficient to prevent
shortage later.

21st November, 1917.—Colonel Williamson
Oswald* went on the 21st November, 1917, by
motor car to El Enab and saw G.O.C. 75th
Division and arranged for a section 60-
pounders to go there from 189 heavy battery.

22nd November, 1917.—Two 60-pounder
guns of 189 H. Battery on the 22nd November,
1917, moved in accordance with the arrangements made with the G.O.C. 75th Division on
the 21st. They remained at or near Kebara,
1½ miles down the hill from Enab along the main
Jaffa to Jerusalem road until early in December, 1917. This is a point on level ground
about two miles west of Kulonieh. From an
observation post on the ridge immediately to
the east of them they could take part in the
struggle of the 75th Division for Jerusalem, and
later were able to support the 60th Division in

---

*With Stewart, Brigade-Major, R.A., XXIst Corps.

this area. The difficulties of the ground had
prevented the heavy artillery, 189 heavy and 380
siege, following the 52nd Division on to its present front; so these two guns were the only
available heavy artillery in the XXIst Corps
struggle round Nebi Samwil. They were
tractor drawn.   On its whole front on 22nd
November, 1917, from the sea, where the Desert
Mounted Corps had no heavy artillery, to the
Kulonieh neighbourhood, the force only had,
besides the above two 60-pounders, two more
60-pounders of 189 heavy battery and four
6-inch howitzers of 380 siege battery, Majors
Richardson and Powell, R.G.A.   These were the
only heavy artillery guns it was found possible
to transport with the advance of the XXIst
Corps after the third Battle of Gaza.   They
were originally allotted to the 52nd Division and
advanced and fought with it.   The 60th Division in its advance brought up 15 heavy battery,
60-pounders; at that time, 1st to 22nd November, it could not have been part of 100th Heavy
Artillery Group, but it appears to have been
detached from the 60th Division about the 22nd
November, 1917.   Further search regarding its
action in the forward struggle is required; this
battery was horsed.

24th November to 29th November, 1917.—On
the 24th November, 1917, the situation was that
the XXIst Corps advance was stopped.   The
XXIst Corps Heavy Artillery, represented by
only two batteries, 189 H.B. and 380 S.B., with

15 H.B. joining as part of the 60th Division of
the XXth Corps, was spread from near Jaffa
to near Kolonieh.   So in the lull the acting
B.G.R.A., Colonel Williamson Oswald, decided
to try and get up more heavy artillery.

At El Kubab, the advanced Corps Headquarters, the G.O.C. XXIst Corps, General
Bulfin, on the 24th-25th November, 1917, informed Colonel Williamson Oswald that there
was to be a change in the situation, and the
XXIst Corps would be replaced by the XXth
Corps at Nebi Samwil (Mizpa) and to the east
and south, for the operation against the
Jerusalem area, while the XXIst Corps would
act from the sea up to the XXth Corps.   The
acting B.G.R.A. asked for the following heavy
artillery, and the Corps Commander concurred:
—Two heavy artillery group headquarters, two
6-inch Mk. VII. guns, 43 siege battery, three
more 60-pounder batteries, and two more 6-inch
howitzer batteries.   On the 28th and 29th
November, 1917, the heavy artillery reinforcements moved off from the neighbourhood of the
Wadi Ghuzze.   This was a severe march, as the
rain had made the roads and tracks to the north
in a soft state in the cotton soil belts, and the
metalled roads were in a bad state of repair.

13th December, 1917.—By the 13th December, 1917, the heavy artillery reinforcements
had arrived in the XXIst Corps area.   At this
period touch with the base was difficult, and for
a short period rations mainly consisted of bully

beef and oranges. The oranges were beneficial
in cases of boils and sores, which had become
common.   The country people began to come
to life, and ploughing and the irrigation of the
orange gardens began again.   A common
ploughing team was a camel and a small
donkey.

The original forward heavy artillery, 189
H.B. and 380 S.B., were in action north of
Selmeh, 380 being in orange gardens with very
little cover.   These batteries about this time
came under heavy artillery orders again.   Also
one sound-ranging section, with the latest in-
struments, came up from Wadi Ghuzze, where
it had acted with the XXIst Corps for the third
Battle of Gaza.   The section took up a position
in front of Surafend and Beit Degan (ancient
Beth Dagon), north of the Jaffa-Ramleh main
road.   It may be noted that there was no
" flash spotting " separate organization with the
XXIst Corps at any time.

CHAPTER 16.

WHEN reinforced, 13th December, 1917, the XXI. Corps possessed for the first time a properly constituted Corps heavy artillery. This consisted of a properly constituted Corps heavy artillery headquarters under a brigadier-general, Colonel Williamson Oswald, with staff (see Note 16), signalling details and transport much as in France. The officers and men mainly came from the old 61st heavy artillery group headquarters; though the acting-brigade-major, Aubrey Thompson, D.S.O., on pending promotion, and W. Matthews, the valued adjutant, because of increasing deafness, had to be reluctantly parted with. There were two group H.A. Headquarters as follows:—100 Heavy Artillery Group on the right or east, with two horsed 60-pounder batteries, 181 and 15, and one 6-inch how. battery, 134; on the left, western or sea flank, was 102 Heavy Artillery Group with two 60-pounder batteries, 189 and 202, both tractor-drawn, and two 6-inch how. batteries, 209 and 380; also at this time 43 S.B.,

which consisted of two 6-inch Mk. VII. guns,
was in 102 H.A. Group.   Of these batteries,
43 S.B., 134 S.B., 209 S.B., and 181 H.B. had
previously fought in Macedonia for about a
year; also 43 S.B., then with 6-inch Mk. VII.,
had been in Gallipoli previously.   Should the
names of batteries be reproduced in any official
history, it is hoped all these eight batteries will
be included; also the 100th and 102nd R.A.
Group had come up, and should be also
included.   Later, in 1918, 95 Heavy Artillery
Group, under Lieutenant-Colonel Moberly,
D.S.O., arrived, having previously fought on the
Italian Front.   On the 1st March, 1918, it was
located at Mulebbis (see Note 17).

7th to 23rd December, 1917.—The situation
at Jaffa, with the enemy holding the right bank
of the River Auja at its mouth, was a peculiar
one.   The British forces had the exceptional
advantage—an advantage scarcely possessed
outside the Turkish Empire—of occupying an
enemy modern town, and in this case well within
range of the enemy's guns, even of his field
artillery.   Jaffa proper had an Arab population
interspersed with Syrians, French, Maltese, and
Greeks, many of whom were absentees, and
whose large and comfortable houses stood in
fertile orange gardens on the outskirts.   To the
north the suburb of Tel Aviv was Jewish.   It
consisted of semi-detached and detached villa
residences, rather of the London suburban
types.   About a mile north of Tel Aviv, and

about two miles from the south bank of the
Auja River, was Sarona, nestling in orange
gardens and vineyards, with shade provided by
well-grown eucalyptus.   The houses in Sarona
lay along a broad dusty road, and were rather
of the tropical bungalow type.   There were
large and well-filled wine cellars.   Sarona had
about twenty houses, and was German, not
German-Jew.   All these places—Jaffa, Tel
Aviv, and Sarona—swarmed with inhabitants,
none of whom were deported until Sarona had
to be emptied owing to a suspicion of spying.
     When the Turks retook the right bank of
the Auja, on 25th November, 1917, those villages
and houses on the north bank which were incor-
porated in the Turkish defences became targets
for British guns, and were pretty well holed.
There was never a single reprisal on the houses
or buildings of Sarona, Tel Aviv, or Jaffa, nor
on the houses near the Auja which were in the
British outpost line.   This negative action on
the part of the enemy is significant of their
mentality.   These valuable properties, being
mostly those of Turkish and German subjects,
were not in any way lessened in value by enemy
action.   This immunity in Jaffa gave the
British a good choice of billets at a very wet
season; but the immunity of Jaffa might not
last, unless the Force by advancing preserved
Jaffa from enemy's shells.
     This question as to the choice to advance or
not to advance is an opportunity for discussing

for a moment how the whole Palestine campaign was regarded by some of its more
humble participants, and how what was in their
minds may have filtered to the general public
and to some in authority.

There were important considerations which
might determine an advance on the Palestine
Front.   At this time the invidious term "side
show" had not come into notice, and the
Palestine Forces considered themselves well
co-ordinated in the main scheme of co-operation
on all Fronts.   It appeared to many minds that
the force in Palestine was pulling its weight
well.   Already it had issued a message of hope
to the Allied Armies and civilian populations by
taking Jerusalem, and it was obtaining results
out of all proportion to the losses sustained
when compared with losses elsewhere.   Again,
to those on the spot, it was obvious that the
Egyptian Expeditionary Force had behind it
the good wishes, and with the good wishes the
potential man-power, of a vast portion of the
habitable globe which Britain's good name had
rallied to the side of the Allies.   It would be
difficult to utilise fully this man-power in the
cold of France, but it could be poured unceas-
ingly into a semi-tropical or even into a South
European campaign, if such a campaign
eventuated after the fall of Turkey.   Africa
and Asia were potential reserves of man-power.
Even South America was becoming stirred.
Also enemy submarines did not exist in the

Southern Ocean to prevent Allied movement and supplies there.

History, too, appeared to give a parallel of very favourable augury. Napoleon said, " It was the Spanish ulcer which destroyed me." Much as under Wellington in Spain and Portugal a decision was gained which counteracted the Napoleonic victories and drawn battles in a crowded Central Europe, so it was hoped that Palestine would lead to a decision which, on the crowded French Western Front, seemed in December, 1917, as far off as ever. Again, the Peninsula campaigns and the Palestine operations had the similarity of being " side shows " under British management exclusively; and let it be remembered that British management implied a staff and an army thoroughly saturated with belief in the advantages of Sea Power—Sea Power a key to success, hardly to be comprehended by continentals: Sea Power which forbids success in a short campaign to a rapidly mobilised army, as Kitchener had well realised.

As the above thoughts passed through minds in Palestine, the Palestine operations did appear of importance, and those engaged there were beginning to see daylight and a foretaste of victory. It is known that hopes of a reasonable chance of success reached some of the junior members of the British Government, who were assured that from the behaviour of the Turks they appeared more ripe for conquest than enemies on other fronts had shown signs of being. Heavy artillery officers had chances of discussion with their heavy artillery comrades on other fronts, and it appeared doubtful if the heavy artillery maxim—that it is the duty of the soldier to kill without being himself unnecessarily killed—was receiving the attention it should in the costly and crowded warfare in some regions elsewhere. In a record of this nature it is as well that it should be known that the soldiers on the spot had these ideas. Later on, about April to July, 1918, the troops were annoyed at the wanton abuse of " side shows " which appeared.

It is as well also that a protest should be on record against the derogatory words put into the new edition of Hamley's " Operations of War," which misses the importance strategically of the purely British-run " side show." Hamley's editor deprecates the necessity of the operations for the destruction of the Turkish Empire. He suggests that less would have been enough, but he does not point out a halfway house between the Suez Canal and Constantinople that would have been safe and satisfactory. The reason is obvious. There was no possible halfway house. The vitality of Turkey since the war goes to prove that.

Having thus cleared the situation to show there was, in the minds engaged with the question, a justification for an advance in Palestine, the record of December, 1917, can be again taken up. In order to facilitate an advance of the Palestine Forces on the whole front of the XXI Corps it was necessary, as a preliminary, to cross the Auja River at or near its mouth. A limited objective was considered. In conjunction with Brig.-General Humphreys, B.G.G.S., the acting B.G.R.A., pointed out that the security of Jaffa from long-range shell fire was advisable, and could be included in the object of the proposed offensive. This was done, and the limited objective as attained, on 23rd December, 1917, will be seen to give a peculiar conformation to the British front. Roughly the front of the XXI. Corps from the Mediterranean at Arsuf (Appolonia) to Rantieh forms the arc of a quarter of a circle centring on Jaffa. In the course of the above operation, after the 52nd Division had attained their magnificent feat of arms in crossing the Auja at and near its mouth in bad weather, the 54th Division followed by storming Bald Hill near Mulebbis, and the advance to the Arsuf-Rantieh line became a comparatively easy affair. The XXI. Corps, following the lines of least resistance, avoided for a time the struggle for the hills south of Mount Ephraim, and consolidated its position in the easier ground of the plain of Sharon; while the arc taken up prevented the enemy from placing their long-range guns within ten miles of the town of Jaffa. Jaffa consequently became sufficiently immune to act as a sea base and a railway centre, and became XXI. Corps headquarters. A light railway, invaluable for ammunition, was pushed across the Auja, and a strong timber bridge was built for caterpillar tractors at Kharbat Hadra, where a ruined dam held up the upper waters of the Auja at about four miles from its mouth. The XXI. Corps also in taking up its lines, both now and in the future advances, was careful to consider the question of observation for artillery purposes. Where in the advances it was possible to impose the will of the British in choosing positions, an excellent front line was taken up, giving the heavy artillery observation a chance of posts commanding the Turkish positions. For this the heavy artillery was grateful.

During the original advance across the Auja, on the 21st December, 1917, the Bible story of the Red Sea crossing had a miniature counterpart: the slight tides of the Mediterranean Sea in conjunction with the Auja current were found to have formed a hard sand-bar at the Auja mouth. This bar was a few yards in the sea and was just covered at low tide, while the high tide raised the sea level only a few inches. This was the causeway over which the tractor-drawn heavy artillery, four 60-pounder guns of 189 heavy battery, on the 22nd December, 1917, followed the 52nd Division, while the struggle north of Kharbat Hadra was still in the balance. The causeway was a difficult one to drive on. Pickets and guide posts were put up, and the

battery got across with the loss of one caterpillar tractor, which became immovable at the
entrance to the causeway and gradually sank
day by day until it entirely disappeared, marked
by a pole.   It was only retrieved some weeks
later in dry weather.   The driving of the caterpillar tractor drivers of the A.S. Corps is
unforgettable to those who saw it; it required
great skill and nerve in a dangerous position,
with the deafening roar ᧒f the tractor's engine
preventing any verbal orders, and with the
danger of drowning ever present if an upset
happened.   Shortly after the heavy battery
had crossed some freak of wind and tide
occurred, and the bar at the Auja mouth disappeared, leaving deep water, thus completing
the Biblical analogy.   However, the needed
support of heavy artillery to the advanced lines
was across the river, and also by this means the
heavy artillery was distributed in depth and
could await the further advance which the
upper Auja crossings later on permitted to more
batteries.   The cover for heavy artillery on the
plain of Sharon and near Mulebbis was scanty.
In the plain the guns were under the cover of
their gun-nets which sufficed, and elsewhere in
orange groves and under eucalyptus and babul
thorn trees.   The flash cover was often very
inadequate as the guns found defilade, that is,
cover, from the high ground to the east difficult
to obtain.   There was no taking up of positions
required from these guns, to enable them to fire

with full 60-pounder charge on our own front line. This had sometimes been insisted on by superior authority elsewhere (page 111), but the existence of reduced charges enabled the Corps Heavy Artillery commander to satisfy the requirements of fire on the front line without sacrificing the really much more common use of 60-pounders, namely, to fire at medium and long ranges. The C.H.A. was grateful for the sanity of outlook which accepted the use of reduced charges, if front-line defence should be wanted from 60-pounder guns; for this very much enlarged the choice of positions, and by giving increased flash cover enabled the batteries to reduce their chances of loss without impairing their necessary role.

The 75th Division on the right of the XXIst Corps on the 11th December, 1917, began an advance from Haditha supported by a section of 134 Siege Battery 6-inch howitzers under Captain Brotherton or Burns (?), R.G.A. This advance ceased on the 22nd December, 1917, for the time. Subsequently the section of 134 S.B. was attached to the 75th Division, which advanced over eight miles of switchback country and brought up the two 6-inch howitzers in the divisional attacks from December till 21st March, 1918, making roads via Abud to the Wadi Deir Ballut. On the 21st March, 1918, mainly by means of the 54th Division at Mejdel Yaba,* and then the 75th Division joining on to

---

*See Note 25.

M

the 10th Division of the XXth Corps, the XXIst
Corps was able to consolidate, with a few minor
adjustments, the line that was held up to the
18th September, 1918.   This line was useful,
both as a jumping-off place for the decisive
battle of the 19th to the 26th September, 1918,
and also as a holding-on position which the
Egyptian Expeditionary Force could occupy
while its constitution was changed to a large
proportion of Indian, some Jewish, British West
Indian and South African, Cape battalions,
with a large force of Indian cavalry and a force
of Indian mountain artillery; when a call for
British battalions and heavy artillery came in
order to fill up the gaps in the fronts in France
and Belgium.   The operation which secured the
Wadi Deir El Ballut was only completed in the
nick of time before the German break-through
which reached nearly to Amiens.   Had the
Palestine Force delayed this most useful
advance the chances of success for the decisive
battle of the 19th September, 1918, might have
been jeoparized, as the line of the Wadi Ballut
was essential.   Without the Wadi Ballut the
heavy artillery would have been able to act
decisively only in the maritime plains, and even
there with insufficient cover from the east.   On
the mountain front of the XXIst Corps their
support would have been weak, as their positions were not advanced until the 21st March
gave the British the Wadi Ballut.   Truly the
advance of March, 1918, to the Wadi Ballut was

a most timely one; its effect, too, was strategically important, and by aiding the victory of 19th September, 1918, it was felt on all fronts. The attachment of the two 6-inch howitzers of 134 Siege Battery gave much support to the 75th Division and helped to quicken its advance. They became for the moment the apple of the eye for the division, and gigantic and successful efforts were made over that rugged country to provide tracks suitable for their caterpillar traction.   Indeed the passage of these caterpillars left the tracks in very good condition for all manner of other vehicles.   This attachment of heavy howitzers to a division contains a valuable lesson; the guns were useful and their possession was a novelty.   The transport required for them did not trench on other transport resources in the division.   Labour, not otherwise available, was very early at hand to push them into the best position.   No doubt, theoretically, the corps could have attained the same results by requisitioning the divisional labour; but there is a psychology in these matters, and the method of temporary attachment gave the needed results very smoothly.

CHAPTER 17.

PREPARATION FOR BATTLE.

PREVIOUS to the 20th July, 1918, a high velocity 15-centimetre (5.9-inch) gun had fired on points inside the XXIst Corps area, which were previously considered to be out of range for any gun known to be on this portion of the enemy's front. It was doubted whether the rounds reported to have been fired had been fired in fact; but on careful enquiry it was found that a shell had fallen on a certain point near Jaffa. This shell had apparently come from the north-east. If the direction, namely, from the north-east, had been correctly guessed, it was clear that the British railhead of the standard-gauge line at Ludd (Lydda) was nearer to this gun than Jaffa, and was therefore vulnerable to this nature of fire. Ludd was at this time a large railway station with some miles of sidings and platforms, where all the " Q " departments (see explanation, page 201) activities could carry on: with metalled roads and yards, with numbers of huts, camps, a casualty clearing station, and with an ordnance department supplying stores and ammunition to the XXI. Corps. The consideration that Ludd was vulnerable to enemy shell was a serious matter in view of the offensive now only a few weeks off.

There had been no indication of the location of the H.V. Gun from the sound-ranging sections, as there was a gap in their catchment area. How the gap was dealt with is a story related for 10th September, 1918. The instrumental flash spotting, undertaken by the O.P.'s in lack of a flash-spotting unit, had not located the gun, which fired at rare intervals and, it was believed, with others. The visibility of the early morning hours at this season was against the British observation, which looked out eastwards and northwards, while southwards and westwards the morning light was clear and advantageous to the enemy. The few rounds fired by this H.V. Gun had in consequence not been caught, as the time chosen for the long-range fire was generally in the morning. On the other hand, the visibility from the British position was very good in the afternoon hours and in the early dusk of evening.

The dusk hours, both morning and evening, were avoided when possible by the British and equally by the enemy, in times of trench warfare, for purposes of artillery fire. The reason was that at dusk it was possible to see both the gun-flash and the country. The flash showed up in the half-light, together with the actual ground features which were in line with the tell-tale flash. In the half-light of evening, for instance, the ground features had not yet melted into the night landscape, and so these features, helped by the visible flash, gave the firing gun away, even when it fired at rare intervals only.

On the 20th July, 1918, in the evening, a report came in to the XXI. Corps counter-battery staff that at 20.00 hours the high-velocity 15-centimetre gun of the enemy had fired one round towards Selme village. The report said that, owing to this fire having occurred in the gloaming, crossbearings had been obtained with ease, and that the H.V. gun was located in K square (see Note 8), namely, at K 27a, 4, 5 (map of Fejja area, 1 in 40,000 squared). This point is near Kharbat Kafr Barah, in the Wadi Kana and north of Kafr Kasin, a distinctly forward position. The Wadi Kana is the great ravine that comes down from Mount Gerizim to Jiljulie (Gilgal) in the plain of Sharon. The action of firing this gun at this hour was noted as remarkable, and it was thought possible that the enemy might see fit to shift the gun. To prevent this the right section of 15 Heavy Battery, 60-pounders, fired 38 rounds H.E. and 24 rounds shrapnel during the night, and the position was kept under observation until 16.00 hours on 21st July, 1918. Then 380 S.B. fired 139 rounds 6-inch how. for destruction, with aeroplane observation, getting 1 " OK," 52 " Z," 17 " Y," 28 "A," and 20 " B." After this no more annoyance was suffered from this long-

range high-velocity gun.   It is conceded that
two rounds were reported at 07.15 hours on the
29th July, and one round at 05.25 on the 1st
August, as fired from a " long-range gun," but
it was not from this 15-centimetre (5.9-inch)
high-velocity gun.

The estimate was justified that the position
of the H.V. gun threatened Ludd Station.   The
location at K 27a, 4, 5, was 12½ miles from the
great station at Ludd, while from the point near
Jaffa, where the round from this gun was reported as having fallen, it is 13½ miles to the gun
position.   So Ludd was well within range.   The
drastic action taken to hold and destroy the
gun appears to have saved the British standard-
gauge rail-head from the gun's attentions.

It may be explained for the benefit of non-
technical readers that, in the XXI. Corps, the
method of shoots for destruction with air
observation was as follows:—

The point on which it was desired to shoot
was marked on an air photograph of the ground
by the counter-battery staff.   The air observer
had to locate this point.   The air observer was
not required to see a hostile battery at this
point, as concealment of the guns might be
complete enough to prevent any sight of them;
also because, on the Palestine hills, all sorts of
features appeared that could deceive an
observer searching for his object.   Of course,
if an observer saw indications that a battery
was elsewhere he should report it.   The

observer, in consequence of these orders, located the point or the points he had been given, and then observed in relation to that point only.   In the present case one direct hit fell on the point ordered to be fired on, also 52 rounds were within a 25-yard circle of the point, namely, those marked " Z," and 17 marked " Y."   All of these may be called destructive (see Notes 11 and 14).   As regards the rest of the notation, " Y " is a circle of 10 yards radius, "A" of 50 yards, and " B " of 100 yards.   The map location of K 27a, 4, 5, means that the gun was located into an area.   K 27 was a square of 1000 yards side; " a " was the left-hand top quarter-square, therefore of 500 yards a side, and this quarter-square was subdivided into ten divisions on each side, so that " 4, 5," gave an intersection which indicated a square of 50 yards a side, where the gun was.   The actual intersection was indicated by the point marked for the air observer to shoot on, and was if necessary notified by co-ordinates, reducing the area to a square of 5 yards a side.   The commander of the British battery that was carrying out the shoot had supplied to him a similar air photograph to that given to the air observer. Each photograph was marked with the point and with circles showing the zones Z, Y, A, and B, while direction was noted by use of the clock-face rule.   At this period it is believed 0 or 12 o'clock was true north, 6 was south, 3 was east, and 9 was west.

One example of a heavy artillery shoot will suffice as a specimen.   201 rounds of 6-inch how. high-explosive shell of 100 lbs. weight were fired on a hostile battery at K 20. c. 1, 2, between the hours of 15.35 and 17.52 by aeroplane observation, and from four guns on the 14th August, 1918, in great heat.   The 6-inch how. of 26 cwt. was the heaviest weapon on the XXI. Corps front for these shoots.

10th September, 1918.—Early in September, 1918, the two sound-ranging sections with the XXI. Corps were distributed roughly as follows:—

Under Captain Gott, R.A., who was also in command of the whole unit, one worked from the Auja river, north of Mulebbis, in an arc westwards to catch gun reports from the sea at Arsuf eastwards to about Kefr Saba.   This was an important area and on the maximum front that one section could stretch to.   There was only one other sound-ranging section available.   This section, under Lieutenant Owen (?), took up a position to catch gun reports from the eastern (right) flank of the XXI. Corps front westwards for about 11,000 yards, namely, from Haris to about Bidie and Mesha.   This region was a ghastly switch-back area of deep ravines running from the main Jerusalem-Samaria ridge, which averages 2000 feet in height, down to the western plains of Yehudie (Jehud) and Sharon, which is something under 400 feet above sea level.   Nestling in these

ravines were the batteries and trenches of both
sides.   The batteries had been brought there
by military tracks descending from the 2000-
feet ridge before mentioned; or uphill by using
the defiladed mouths of the ravines where they
debouched on the western plains of Yehudie
and Sharon.   Auxiliary tracks were made over
the ridges to facilitate advance and retreat
north and south; and, for supply purposes, a
British light railway came to Lubban.

This was, then, the position early in September, 1918.   One valuable lateral artery for
British supply was a deep canyon called Wadi
Ballut.   Starting from the good military road
from Ludd to Mejdel Yaba (Aphek), the track
skirts the south edge of Mejdel Yaba, with its
prominent Crusader's castle, and goes eastward
up the wadi, leaving the maritime plain behind
it.   The gradient is easy and the sides of the
wadi are at first sloping, but ultimately the
ravine becomes a gorge with a depth of some
600 feet, of which the northerly sides are the
most precipitous.   This wadi was a hot spot
at times, but owing to its extent and depth it
was always possible to count on its being
traversable for all kinds of transport.   Judging
from the British side of the terrain, it was con-
cluded that enemy artillery positions were
possible and perhaps numerous in the higher
or eastern portion of the mountain region in
front of the XXI. Corps.   The eastern sound-
ranging section of the XXI. Corps was usefully

employed in this labyrinth of ravines which
borders Mount Ephraim.   As, however, the
British plans of attack for the battle of the 19th
September, 1918, developed, and as the knowledge of possible positions for artillery
increased, it became apparent that in the more
rolling area from the western mouths of the
ravines up to the commencement of the precipitous canyons, namely, from Jiljulie (Gilgal)
to Bidie and Mesha, there was an important
locality as suitable for enemy heavy and other
guns, as the British had found the corresponding locality on their side of the front line.   This
area had not disclosed many hostile guns.
Should a number of hostile guns be concealed
there they could make a surprise opening in the
coming battle.   Such a surprise opening would
make these concealed guns immune to the
British counter-battery neutralisation at first
(see explanation, page 199), and even later the
neutralisation could not be very thorough for
some time.   These surprise artillery positions
are inevitable, but the aim is to make them as
few as possible by previous discovery.   It
seemed urgent to clear up this uncertainty.   So
with great rapidity the XXIst corps, eastern,
or right, sound-ranging section was moved towards the debouchment of the Wadi Ballut into
the plain.   The new position had a very exposed
line of observation, well forward of the villages
of Mejdel Yaba and Deir Ballut.   The headquarters were in the Wadi Ballut, about 2000

yards east of Mejdel Yaba village. Now it has been said that the Wadi Ballut was a hot spot at times, and the erection of the headquarters of this sound-ranging section coincided with some enemy shelling by 5.9-inch howitzers, but the position was well chosen and escaped damage. The section was ready for work on the 10th September, 1918, or latish on the night of the 9th/10th September.

An interesting series of events then took place. The 54th Division chose the night of the 10th/11th September, 1918, to push out some patrols of an exceptional nature; also the O.C. 102 Heavy Brigade says that there was a partial bombardment from the British further to the west. The result of these acts was that during the night of 10th/11th September, 1918, the enemy opened artillery fire at 22.15 to 22.30, at 01.55 to 02.01, and at 02.05 to 02.20 hours, and in consequence the XXIst Corps eastern sound-ranging section, within some 24 hours of being ready in its new position, made the important discovery that there did exist north of Mejdel Yaba a considerable number of enemy guns, which up to then had not been disclosed, nor of which there was any previous evidence.

Apparently what had happened was as follows:—The enemy had heard, and had also come into contact with, the British Infantry in the debatable ground among the low hills north of Mejdel Yaba. The patrolling seemed to his front-line troops to presage a serious attack,

and consequently the carefully hidden barrage
of the enemy was put down with its whole
power.   A disclosure of that kind is always
possible; but think of the lost opportunity had
not the sound-ranging section been in position
to catch the gun reports and record them.   The
smartness of the section in getting into position
can be a matter of congratulation.   The correct
appreciation of the location of these totally
hidden and hitherto silent guns can be well
credited to the commander of this sound-
ranging section and to the counter-battery
organization of the XXIst Corps.   The discovery was tactically important.   These barrage
batteries were so placed as to cover and destroy
the hinge of the great wheel of the purposed
attack of the reinforced XXIst Corps about to
take place on the 19th September, 1918.

A glance at the map will show that the wheel
of the XXIst Corps hinged on its right flank
near Ballut and about 16 miles from its sea
flank.   The guns disclosed were in the squares
K, L, M and N of the squared map (see note 8),
that is, east and south-east of the village of
Jiljulie.   The guns consisted of nine 4.2-inch
howitzers in four positions; four 75-mm. guns
in two positions, and six 5.9-inch howitzers in
three positions: in all of 19 guns in nine positions.   The catch was valuable, as it disclosed
four times the number of 5.9-inch howitzers
previously recorded in this area; while of lesser
natures it disclosed more than a 25 per cent.

addition to the known 4.2-inch and smaller natures.

To go into figures, it may here be noted that the XXIst Corps counter-battery list of suspected positions of enemy guns early in September, 1918, worked out to 25 positions containing 56 guns, including thirteen 5.9-inch howitzers for XXIst Corps front. The revised list on which the neutralization was based for the battle of the 19th September, 1918, was as follows:—On the west or left counter-battery area, which is outside the present story, there were listed 31 positions or 58 guns, including eleven 5.9-inch howitzers and four 4.2-inch guns, with the remaining 43 mainly distributed among 4.2-inch howitzers and 75-mm. guns. On the east or right counter-battery area to which this story refers there were listed 21 positions of 55 guns, including eight 5.9-inch howitzers, two 4.2-inch guns, and 45 others, namely, 4.2-inch howitzers and 75-mm. guns.

On the 19th September, 1918, the hostile barrage fire was formidable enough on the 54th Division and the French Detachment which formed the hinge of the XXIst Corps attack, yet the fact that the corps knew of these positions, but had given no sign to alarm them and to induce them to change their locations, contributed greatly to simplify the British counter-battery neutralization at the commencement of the battle.

Now, were the story to stop here, the reader

might join his thoughts to those of an able and popular leader of high military rank who had not been in the Palestine campaign. This officer, listening to a lecture where the deeds of heavy artillery were being " boosted " rather in the present style, proceeded to apply an antidote. It is presumed that as the audience was mainly junior infantry officers, the popular leader aforesaid sought to cheer them up. His antidote consisted of a story from the Western Front. The story was that after much bombardment of a suspected German gun position near Lille in 1918, the people responsible for the bombardment advanced to pick up the pieces and to count the hits. They were met by an indignant occupier of a farm, who, in answer to their inquiries on the subject, made the following reply:—" No, messieurs, I know not nor have I ever heard that the place you mention has ever been occupied by a German battery. This, however, I do know: that in your recent furious bombardment of that field," pointing in quite a different direction, " your guns have killed my ass."

With all respect to the distinguished narrator of the above, and with sincere condolences for the Western Front concerned, in Palestine also it had been found possible to check the effect of the British fire, and luckily for the present narrative a very different result had been elicited. The actual ground in question in squares K, L, M and N, as well as other localities, was gone over, and some perfectly good and genuine photographs of some of the enemy gun positions referred to are in existence, showing the destruction wrought by the British shells. Together with a message of thanks from the G.O.C. 54th Division, these photographs go to show that the neutralizing fire of the XXIst Corps heavy artillery in the Battle of Sharon of the 19th September, 1918, did find the enemy guns in several positions where they had been theoretically located by the sound-ranging section.

August and September, 1918.—The preparations for the Battle of Sharon, 19th September, 1918, were carried out with secrecy. All that was given out was: "The corps front is to be advanced." The cover for the necessary tactical moves on the open plains was very small. To harbour by day the reinforcing heavy and siege batteries coming from the XXth Corps area (see note 21), all that were available for cover were a few trees near Surafend and a few trees at Sarona, where the caterpillar tractors and guns of successive battery after battery hid by day. They went forward and came into action under their gun nets, made like great fishing nets, of about 1½ inch or 2 inch rope, and with about a foot mesh. These nets were found the most adequate cover in this land, and also, strangely enough, kept the flies away. The tractors, after unlimbering their guns in their battle positions, parked back with the corps tractors and so were not noticed. These batteries were not allowed to fire at all until the surprise attack commenced on the 19th September, 1918. Survey operations had been conducted to give them accuracy for the surprise attack.

Balloon reconnaisance was undertaken in August and gave the C.H.A. Commander some idea of the small undulations in rear of the Turkish positions which might act as rallying points. These reconnaissances may have raised suspicion, as the enemy paid special attention to destroying the balloons. The necessary view points are best gained by holding the balloon steady at various heights, say from 800 feet upwards, by which the folds of the ground reconnoitred can be appreciated. This is better than raising the balloon to its maximum height and reconnoitring there, as this latter method gives too featureless and too flat a view.

As regards the XXIst Corps Heavy Artillery, only the Commander and his brigade major, Major Bagnall, R.G.A., knew the plan, and so on them devolved the whole detail of minor matters. This precaution of secrecy was taken in all formations. It says much for the technical knowledge of the superior officers in the corps that it was possible to insist on so few persons knowing the plan of the higher command until a very advanced date—in most cases until the attack was launched. Included in the arrangements for which the Corps Heavy Artil-

N

lery was responsible were the future moves of
the tractor and lorry transport of the heavy
artillery and the amount of transport it would
be possible to detach for the purpose of a forward move of the troops other than the heavy
artillery.   The scheme decided upon was the
detachment of practically the whole transport
of the heavy artillery, except that required for
guns moving with the advance. Much experience had been gained in the rapid move of the
Force after the third Battle of Gaza. It was
on that experience that it was decided to move
two heavy artillery brigade headquarters as
well as batteries; also the units of transport
were provided with petrol, oil, grease, water
and rations on a scale—namely, 5 per cent. on
their total load—that would free them from
indenting for some days. In these matters of
transport the advice of Major Sanders, the
senior officer R.A.S.C., attached heavy artillery,
was sought, though necessarily even he could
not be consulted till very shortly before the
battle. While on the subject of R.A.S.C. transport it may be mentioned that the higher
authorities of that corps had intentions of occasionally transferring officers from attachment
to the heavy artillery to other R.A.S.C. (then
Army Service Corps) units. As each such
transfer meant that a new officer had to learn
his heavy artillery supply duties and the special
wants of moving heavy guns and their ammunition, the loss of efficiency to the artillery was

pointed out.   After that very few changes were
made except at the request of the Corps Heavy
Artillery.   Only one such request can be remembered.   This settlement of the question of
transfer was popular with both R.G.A. and
R.A.S.C. officers and led to efficiency.

Various ruses were employed by the Corps
to deceive the local inhabitants as to the time
and place of any probable attack.   One such
ruse was that the townspeople of Jaffa received
a warning to prepare lists of billets for the
XXIst Corps in the ensuing winter, as much
accommodation might be wanted.   This caused
some   pleasurable   excitement   among   the
younger inhabitants and was gossiped about,
as intended.

The completion of the heavy artillery concentration for Sharon found on the XXIst
Corps front 79 guns of the heavy artillery,
namely, twenty 60-pounders, two 6-inch Mk.
VII. guns, two 8-inch howitzers, fifty 6-inch
howitzers, three 4.7-inch guns from coast
defence at Jaffa, and two 15-centimetre (5-9-
inch) captured enemy howitzers (see notes 18,
19, 20, 21).

CHAPTER 18.

19TH September, 1918.—The frontage of the British and Allied attack at the Battle of Sharon at 4.30 a.m. on the 19th September, 1918, by the XXIst Corps was about 16 to 17 miles; for demonstration purposes say 16 miles. In choosing this frontage the higher authorities' scheme fitted in well with the ideas of the Corps Heavy Artillery as regards gaining immunity for the attacking infantry from enemy artillery fire. This may be explained as follows. In any infantry attack the ideal would be that no infantry was subjected to the hostile barrage fire of any guns beyond those in their immediate front; every hostile gun that can switch from its own immediate front on to the front attacked is an additional obstacle to the infantry attack.

Assuming that the enemy heavy guns are placed so that their average oblique fire at their average extreme ranges can reach a point on the front they are defending of four miles, say, right and left of their central line of fire; the amount of concentration these guns can attain on parts of the line not directly in front of their central line of fire can be easily calculated. Take the simplest case: all guns under the above conditions on a line of position eight miles long could concentrate at one point in the centre of their 8-mile front should it require defence. Again, all the guns under the above conditions on a line of positions twelve miles long could concentrate their fire on the central four miles of their 12-mile front. An attack on a 4-mile front might therefore expect to be fired on from hostile guns stretching on a line of twelve miles; to put it otherwise, an attack on a 4-mile front might have to endure a barrage 200 per cent. extra to the barrage normally produced by the hostile heavy artillery on the immediate front attacked. Where the front of attack is greater and greater than four miles under the above conditions the extra percentage of hostile barrage to be endured becomes less and less than the above 200 per cent.

In calculating the avoidance of a concentrated heavy artillery barrage fire likely to be endured, taking the probable hostile armament and its positions, the advantage of making one flank of the attack coincide with the sea was that no concentration of hostile fire could be expected from that side. The concentration of hostile barrage fire by heavy artillery on the eastern, or land flank, was limited to roughly a four to five mile front; so that on about 12 miles of a 16-mile front, that is on 75 per cent.

of the attack, including the seven mile portion marked lightly held, but on which the enemy barrage was bound to fall in their initial defence, no more than the normal frontal barrage was to be endured. In consequence, from a heavy artillery point of view, the selection of so broad a front of attack was regarded as giving much immunity to the British infantry from concentrated enemy heavy artillery fire. The coastwise division, the 60th, and the one next, the 7th Meerut Division, which were the two with most ground to cover, were specially immune from any but frontal fire. The brunt of the concentrated fire from outside the front attacked would be on the troops at the hinge of the right wheel of the XXIst Corps. These troops had the shortest distance to go and would occupy the hostile barrage on their immediate front, while the fire from the east could not do more than concentrate on them and could not reach the divisions making the outer wheel. This was what did happen so far as it has been possible to judge the hostile heavy artillery fire. The successful break-through of the 60th and 7th Meerut Divisions, followed by the cavalry mass and the hard task of the hinge, seem therefore to corroborate the estimate that a very suitable frontage for attack was chosen on this occasion so far as the hostile heavy artillery conditions were concerned.

On the British side, by moving up reinforcing batteries, a great local concentration of heavy artillery against the enemy opposite the XXIst Corps front took place. The gun power was specially strong on the front from the sea along the front of the 60th and 7th Meerut Division, and to a lesser degree along the front of the next attacking division. This local heavy artillery concentration made it possible for the XXIst Corps Heavy Artillery to neutralize the fire of the hostile batteries on an overwhelming scale. All known gun positions were fired on from the opening of the attack and reinforcing guns were ready to take on batteries of the enemy found to be still in action against the attack. This neutralization had been ruled to be the main duty of the XXIst Corps Heavy Artillery, though in addition, but as a secondary duty, a creeping barrage (see explanation page 200) and fire elsewhere had been undertaken if gun strength permitted.

Certain heavy artillery Back Blocks (see explanation page 200) were arranged in conjunction with the attacking divisions. These Back Blocks were to prevent enemy reinforcements and were also provisional S.O.S. to be fired as a barrage if called for by advancing divisions in case these divisions were stopped. They were introduced to act as a variant to the creeping heavy artillery barrage if that barrage moved too quickly. These barrages are not recorded as having been fired, but there was a liaison between the heavy artillery and the advancing divisions until these divisions outstripped the heavy artillery ranges; for instance, the attack on the strong Jiljulie position was supported by the 95th Heavy Artillery Brigade.

A surprise attack on the enemy railhead near the village of Kalkilieh was fired from one 6-inch Mk. VII. gun named " Lizzie." This gun was moved up close to Mejdel Yaba in order to get within range of the railhead, but its power was not disclosed prematurely. It fired on the 19th September, 1918, from Zero plus 60 minutes and for one hour, that is from 5.30 a.m. to 6.30 a.m. The range was nearly the extreme range, namely, 17,000 yards, nearly 10 miles. An examination of railhead afterwards showed that this fire had been successful in making hits on the area of railhead and on the road approaching it. The timing of this attack was arranged so as not to give too early warning to the Turkish higher staffs of the serious nature of the battle.

The initial rates of fire for the heavy artillery barrage were: for the first ten minutes one round per gun per minute; then fifty rounds per gun per hour. The infantry calculated they could advance at the rapid rate* of 100 yards per minute, and the lifts were calculated at this rate. There was no preliminary bombardment. Counter-battery neutralization was as follows: for the first fifteen minutes intense rate at 20 rounds per gun, commencing from Zero hour,

---

* See Note 11.

4.30 a.m. 19th September, 1918; then fifty
rounds per gun per hour. It is reported that by
6.25 a.m. the enemy artillery fire was dimin-
ished.

The ammunition brought up for the Battle
of Sharon was 21,700 rounds for 79 heavy guns
and howitzers on the XXIst Corps front. The
expenditure on these lines for the first hour
would be 4158 rounds, by which time the lifts
would have given 6000 yards increase of range
to the heavy artillery creeping barrage. There
may be in existence documents to show the
exact amount which was fired, but in the
absence of such documents it may be estimated
that double the above amount, say 8300, were
fired up to, say, 7.0 a.m. Take another 200
rounds after this time. The total would be 8500
rounds for 79 heavy guns. After the battle
some 13,000 rounds would have to be retrieved
and replaced in store. "That is the worst of
these victories."

Arrangements had been made for advancing
heavy artillery with the advancing divisions.
The experience of their usefulness in the advance after the third Battle of Gaza induced an
increase to be made. Two brigade headquarters were detailed with a portion of their
batteries so far as transport was available.
These brigades were called for between 08.00
and 10.00 hours by their advancing divisions.

With the 60th Division there advanced 102
Heavy Artillery Brigade, Lt.-Col. Hutchison,

D.S.O., R.G.A., and 91 Heavy Battery, with horses, and 380 Siege Battery with caterpillar tractors.   On the 20th September, 1918, after a very exhausting march, in which over very light friable sandy soil the caterpillar tractors did best, these batteries reached Tul Keram.   By this time, using a large force of Sikh Pioneers and Egyptians, a motor track had been made from the British road at Ras El Ain, ancient Anti Patris, through a thick jungle of thistles in No Man's Land to the Turkish metalled road near Kalkilieh.   By this road, which he had reconnoitred on the afternoon previously, the C.H.A. commander reached the 102nd H.A. Brigade at Tul Keram.   At his instance the G.O.C. 60th Division, Major-General J. Shea, pushed both batteries of the brigade to Anebta, though both men and animals suffered greatly from thirst.   Owing to this advance 91 H. Battery was able to fire 40 rounds of 60-pounder shell during the night of 20th/21st September, 1918.   The objective was eastward, at the main road near Messudieh station on the Turkish railway, in order to block the retreating enemy and into an area not yet reached by British mounted troops.   Anebta was only lightly held by the 60th Division at the time, but it was decided to risk these heavy guns so far forward.   In the mind of the C.H.A. commander, it seemed that eight part-worn guns was not much to risk.

The ultimate result of the action of the

" pincers " in reaching up to the road Jerusalem to Samaria to Nazareth was that the enemy was forced to descend into the Jordan valley east of Nablus (Sechem) prematurely and by a bad road. This road became a shambles.

It is not claimed that these 40 rounds of 60-pounder shell had any material effect, but with the whole force straining to close the northern " pincers " on the Turks, it was up to the long-range artillery to make every effort to co-ordinate with the other arms. The moral effect can be imagined upon the demoralized tail of the enemy's army, when they saw hostile shell of a heavy calibre dropping in their neighbour-hood. The tail probably considered themselves very safe indeed except from the air, and some of them may have been entitled to the epithet *embusques*. Certainly the resultant jambs of lorries and other details in the gorges of the Jordan further eastward go to prove that in their desire to avoid the Messudieh direction the Turkish rear details, practically hurled themselves down a precipice. No part of an army is more vulnerable than these long communication lines, which in the ordinary way are only subject to air bombing, and none are so liable to panic when a real live enemy threatens to appear on the ground.

These 40 rounds were the last heavy artillery fire of the XXIst Corps. The 102 Heavy Artillery Brigade, joined on the 26th September, 1918, by 15 H.B. at Tul Keram, moved as far as

Haifa, and some 60-pounders of 91 H.B. took up the role of coast defence there.

On the 19th September, 1918, the 95th Heavy Artillery Brigade headquarters with 181 heavy battery 60-pounders and 304 siege battery 6-inch howitzers, under Lieut.-Colonel Moberly, D.S.O., R.G.A., advanced.   This brigade supported the attack on the strong enemy works at Jiljulieh and further to the east on the slopes of Mount Ephraim and Azzun, fire on which ended their activity for the war.

The usefulness of the heavy artillery organization continued, as much of their transport was employed in the further pursuit which finished in the submission of Turkey.

The War Diary of the XXIst Corps Heavy Artillery for September, 1918, Appendix 3, gives the course of the Battle of Sharon from minute to minute as reported by the heavy artillery (see note 8).

EXPLANATION OF TECHNICAL TERMS.

COUNTER-BATTERY duties mean the duties of knowing where the enemy's guns are hidden. These enemy's guns can then either be destroyed or can be neutralized.

NEUTRALIZATION means bringing a fire of shells upon the enemy's guns so that he is not able to use them, or can only use them with great loss of power.

DESTRUCTION OF A BATTERY means firing so many heavy shells at it that it has to go out of action until repaired behind the lines.

O.P. means the peep-hole at some exposed place in the trenches or near the trenches from which an artillery officer can direct his guns by signal or telephone or wireless to fire at the enemy. Full words are observation post.

SHOOTING A BATTERY means the orders the officer who is watching the enemy gives to his guns in order to make the guns hit the enemy with their shells. This officer may be in an O.P. or in an aeroplane or in a balloon.

S.O.S., or "Save our Souls," is a term borrowed from ships. In the Army it is the signal by which our troops, generally our infantry, signalled to our artillery, to help them when they, the infantry, were suddenly attacked.

This help was generally given by the artillery barrage.

THE ARTILLERY BARRAGE consisted of a rapid fire of shells fired from the guns behind the infantry and directed so that these shells fell just in front of our infantry, and so struck the enemy's attacking troops or prevented them from coming further forward without great loss. Our shells were directed to fly over the heads of our infantry without hitting them. *A creeping barrage* was one that moved forward at a fixed rate so as to keep just in front of our own advancing infantry and prevent the enemy from firing at them with impunity.

A BACK BLOCK was an artillery barrage arranged to be fired at some points behind the enemy's line to prevent him from using that part of his ground without losing a number of his men.

REGISTRATION means the process by which the range or distance of an object from a gun or guns is found out, often by trial shots. When found the facts are recorded or "registered," giving all necessary data requisite for opening fire again at the said object. If properly registered the freshly opened fire should have a reasonable chance of hitting the object or to be so near it as to "neutralize" it.

CATERPILLAR is a name given to powerful tractors for heavy guns. They were driven by an endless chain, having pieces which gripped the ground as the endless chain went round, and so moved the machine over almost all natures of ground.   Later the " Tank " was invented, which moved in the same way, while its driver and crew were protected by the vehicle being covered with armour.

THE GENERAL STAFF means that part of the Army which thinks out and plans operations in case of a war, or which during a war plans how the work is to be done with a view to ultimate victory.   It is called " G " branch.

" A " *Branch* means the part of the Army that provides the officers and men and which looks after their behaviour.

" Q " *Branch* means the part of the Army which arranges for the movement and welfare of the Army including their food and weapons.

NOTES.

Note 1, page 11.—Others of 61 Heavy Artillery group headquarters were Brown, Earnshaw, Godfrey, Grover, Macdonald, Walker. (See note 12.)

Note 2, page 20.—The old-time rank of Brigadier-General has suffered temporary eclipse. It is of respectable age. Wolfe was a Brigadier-General and temporary Major-General when he took Quebec. Near the end of Edward VII.'s reign the rank was restored. It proved a useful rank, especially during the War 1914 to 1918. British Brigadier-Generals with detachments were in a position to enforce their wishes as Generals among a concourse of Allies. The rank of Colonel Commandant is a new one in its present use. Colonel on the Staff in past generations never had much prestige. In big armies, Continental and elsewhere, Colonel was understood as a commander of a big regiment, but the English language as spoken in the British Army has decreed that the words " The Colonel " mean the officer commanding a battalion of a thousand men or its equivalent. Consequently British human nature decided that the honour of passing from Lieutenant-Colonel to full Colonel was a matter not much worth striving for, especially as it did not mean advance to Major-General, which was reserved for Staff College trained people. In the earlier years of this century such thoughts must have occupied the minds of the authorities. With a great war possible they could not offer Majors and Lieutenant-Colonels sufficient inducement to qualify for higher positions, except the somewhat low inducements of more pay and a little more pension. So a

202

move was made, and a Warrant* was made out giving a new rank in the Army higher than that of Colonel, and this document was put forward for high signature. The signature was obtained, but so well, it is presumed, was the august signatory versed in the tongue of our nearest Ally that he prevented the rank of Corporal (in French Brigadier) being placed above that of Colonel in the British Service. With a stroke of the pen, it is reported, he added General to the wording of the document, which had called the new rank Brigadier. He is reported to have said at the same time, " The rank is Brigadier-General."

Note 3, page 63.—The batteries of the 112th Brigade R.F.A. were placed—A, near Delennele Farm: B, Soyer Farm; C, Le Flauque Farm; D, at Mortlette Chapelle, Le Biset. Major Thomas, 14th Heavy Battery, was in touch, belonging to 16th Heavy Brigade R.G.A., commanded by Colonel Palmer.

Note 4, page 85.—It appears strange how sometimes successful soldiers are tempted to take risks that are not necessary. For instance, take that successful officer, General Symons. Symons was marching with Oswald, who was conducting a convoy on the Indian North-West Frontier in 1898. Oswald was sending some of the Argyll and Sutherland Highlanders up to picket the heights while the convoy marched through a narrow pass on the road. Symons, said "I don't want those pickets out." Then, turning to Oswald, he said, "I don't want to worry the men." It was a risk, but it came off. Later on, in 1899, in the South African War, while conducting operations north of Ladysmith, Symons was shot by the Boers, and his column was badly knocked about. Oswald wondered if adequate precautions were taken by this very gallant officer on that day.

---

* or some such document.

o

Note 5, page 54.—No. 6 Bombay Mountain Battery, now Jacob's, had during Williamson Oswald's command, as subalterns, Chapman, de Brett, H. W. M. Parker, O'Connor, Swinton, Colville, Carey, all good men and capable of getting on with the war when it came, which each one did in his respective sphere. There were also Lieuts. Angus and Sargeaunt, who were killed, Angus before the war, in Africa. The Indian officers were war-experienced. Imam Buksh, Surmukh Singh, Nagina Singh, as were the other ranks, which contained many " Indian Orders of Merit" given for bravery. In the case of the Havildar Major Mohamed Ismail there was a future King's Orderly Officer, who was present in that capacity when King George V. was crowned. Mohamed Ismail was away in London on this very distinguished duty when his new battery, No. 32 Mountain, was in Persia in the coronation year. This battery's shells were the first fired in anger by King George V.'s land forces in his reign (see page 88). In May, 1911, also, two guns of 32 M.B. fired what was known later as a creeping barrage to support attacking infantry. Verily, there is nothing new under the sun.

Note 6, page 92.—For purpose of manufacturing more guns, one gun complete, and serviceable with its carriage, ammunition, and equipment, is sufficient. The manufacturer can go ahead with construction, as he has the requisite details to work from.

Note 7, page 129.—In conversation with a neutral whom Oswald also met during the War in Salonika, this gentleman said that, from his experience in Salonika, he considered the French policy of keeping a force therein in touch with Balkan affairs was sound, as the Bulgars were never out-and-out pro-German, and were always a menace to the German cause should things go wrong, and that this was confirmed by the

Bulgars leaving the German side first. A Bulgar gave Oswald a few years ago the, same expression of opinion. He was an enemy telephonist at Uskub in 1916. He said the pro-German majority in Bulgaria was small. Further confirmation of Balkan mentality comes indirectly from the Servians, who, when brought to fight at Florina, which was outside the then frontier of Servia, said that they did not want to fight for Macedonia, which was the affair of Greece.* In short, all the Balkan nations were in need of some moral push to keep them on one side of the fence or the other, and this push Sarrail's force gave, to the detriment of the Germans.

Note 8, pages 140, 142, 152, etc.—Certain maps, etc., are referred to in the Palestine chapters, the absence of which do not affect this narrative.

Note 9, page 145.—Balloon officers with Beaufoy included Granger, Simons, Booth, Kemps, Naysmyth, Whitehead, Cotton, Todd, Wallace, Thompson.

Note 10, pages 105, 153.—Other Army Service Corps officers with Artillery transport were Baker, Blunt, Colbourne, Cross, Dene, Duncan, Foulger, Harrison, Maple, Templeton, Tracy (see Note 13).

Note 11, page 178, etc.—The distances are believed to be correctly stated.

Note 12, pages 11, 129.—These are the names of the men of 61 Heavy Artillery Group Headquarters. So far as can be ascertained, the date of the list is shortly before the group left Macedonia for Palestine, namely, August, 1917. These men were of a variety of callings before joining for the Great War. For instance, clerk, chairmaker, groom, house decorator, porter, hairdresser, miner, farm labourer, postman, motor driver, student, valet, boot salesman, general post office

*From a Servian source,

telephone instrument inspector, workhouse master, cloth designer, fitter, policeman, cotton piecer. They came from such varied parts of England as Manchester, Northampton, Rochdale, High Wycombe, Warkworth, Kent, Devon, Wigan, London, Lincoln, Brighton, Gravesend, Kenilworth, Leigh, Oldham, Liverpool, Rotherham, Birmingham, York, Brinton, Hull, Sheffield, Sussex, also Glasgow. Brigade-Sergeant-Major Beaven and Sergeant Colmer belonged to the old Army. The rest were mostly Derby Volunteers, and served in the following duties:—As clerks, Hollins, Lawton; as drivers and grooms, Toon, Batton, Anguin, Tyler, Simpson, Walton, Smith, only four at one particular time; as medical orderlies, Westwood, Brewer, Brown; as batmen, doing other work as well, Stephens, Dobson, Davies; as wheeler, Davis; as gunners, with two for Royal Army Medical Corps duties, Lynes, Murdock, Heath, Blackmore, Allum, Meades; as telephonists, Abbott, Etchells, Warn, Ridley, Clark, Crewdson, Galvin, Gibbs, James, Nash, Taylor; on water duty, Butcher, Sullivan; as motor and lorry drivers, Spicer, Stapeley, Sharpe; as motor cyclist, Somervell; Artillery clerk's section, Sergeant Martin; whilst others were Hough, Ridgeley, Bailey. The total was 43, and some very varied duties, with certainly a hundred miles of field telephone wire, and probably much more, to be kept in order during quiet as well as during battle periods. For sudden moves, notes show that an advance party of eight telephonists, three batmen, two clerks, two medical orderlies, one Royal Army Medical Corps man, and one cook were organised.

Note 13, page 153.—The Army Service Corps Companies of mechanical transport attached to the XXI. Corps Heavy Artillery, during the advance of the Corps to the line north of Jaffa and Jerusalem, were engaged in special duties. At this time they were doing much work for ammunition supply of the three Army Corps, the XX., XXI., and Desert Corps. This work included dragging ammunition over miles of heavy sand on improvised sleighs. About 18th November, 1917, there were, according to note-books, at Deir Sineid 811 Company, with one sleigh and nine tractors; 955 Company, two tractors, with two trucks with caterpillar tracks; 988 Company, with one sleigh and eight tractors; 989 Company, with one sleigh and eight tractors, under Captains Bradley and Foulger. They had also some 23 wagons and some workshops. At Wadi Sukerier there was no workshop, but 984 Company, with one sleigh and eight tractors; 1007 Company, with one sleigh eight tractors, and some wagons, under a captain.

At Bela and on the old Gaza front were Captains Phayre (?), Lieutenant Halley, and Lieutenant Brookes, with some of 955 Company, with one sleigh and three tractors; 980 Company; 981 Company, with one sleigh and ten tractors; 1006 Company, with one sleigh and eight tractors; 1008 Company, with one sleigh and eight tractors and some 19 wagons. Also at Bela, with Captain Boyle, were all the repairable wagons, some 90, and workshops. 380 Siege Battery seems to have had 952 Company, with six tractors and some 16 wagons, and 189 Heavy Battery had ten tractors and some ten wagons of 904 Company; these two batteries were fighting and moving with the 52nd Division. About 19th November, 1917, they required immediately, and were sent with Captain Borton to 189 Heavy Battery 110 high explosive and 90 shrapnel shell, this battery having on hand at the time 118 high explosive and 114 shrapnel shell; also to 380 Siege Battery were sent 150 high explosive shell with 60 more to follow, this battery having at the time 180 high explosive 6-inch shell.

Meanwhile the transport of ammunition by sea coastwise on the Mediterranean from Bela to the landing places of Wadi Hesi, Wadi Sukerier, and later Jaffa, carried on during the winter of 1917-1918. The allowance was three ship loads, each calculated at a load of 780 tons, per each fortnight, and the steamer " Proton " did most of this. This was a dangerous job, as a Royal Navy monitor was blown up with all hands at Bela by submarines in November, 1917. The Raratonga* New Zealand detachment did most of the surf landing. For calculation, a ton of ammunition was taken as any of the following, and the loading at Bela depended upon the wants of the fighting troops day by day. A ton was either 28,000 small-arm ammunition, that is, rifle cartridges; or 78 rounds, shell, cartridge, and fuse for the 18-pounder R.F.A. gun; or 100 rounds for the 13-pounder R.H.A. gun; or 100 rounds for the 2.75-inch mountain gun; or 100 rounds for the 13-pounder anti-aircraft gun; or 45 rounds for the 4.5-inch R.F.A. howitzer; or 30 rounds for the 60-pounder R.G.A. gun; or 20 rounds for the 6-inch R.G.A. howitzer; or 18 rounds for the 6-inch Mark VII. R.G.A. gun; or 66 rounds for the 3.7-inch mountain howitzer; or 870 hand grenades (infantry bombs); or 168 rounds of " Stokes " mortar (bombs for firing from trench mortars).

Major Hilder's ammunition party was moving this quantity inland and by lorry (and by rail a little); 690 tons was going to Junction Station (in this crucial fortnight?). End of November, 1917, there was great pressure owing to the ammunition required to push the Turks back on Jerusalem; they were fighting obstinately. According to note-books Major Hilder's party was located about 19th November, 1917:—Captain Stovel in charge of posts; Captain Bradley in charge of tractors; Captain Ward, 905 A.S.C., and

---

* Some fought in the third battle of Gaza in 10 Heavy Battery.

Lieutenant Adams, 905 A.S.C., at Junction Station, where there was a lorry repair workshop; Second Lieutenant Brookes, 981 A.S.C., Captain Lay, 988 Company Army Service Corps, at Junction Station, also Captains Oliver and A. Barnes are shown there. Other A.S.C. companies, apparently with lorries, were also engaged on this work. Captain French with 951, Captain Doyne with 964, Captain Shaw with 965, Captain Lumsden with 982, Captain Murdock with 990 Company. Major Sanders's Staff Officer was Morriss (see pages 188, 212).

Speaking of lorries, a further note shows that the 3-ton lorry (that is, with 3-ton carrying capacity) could carry 52 rounds for the 6-inch guns and howitzers, and 70 rounds for the 60-pounders; the four-horsed general service wagons carried 15 rounds for 6-inch and 40 rounds* for 60-pounder guns. This was first done in Macedonia, and 25 per cent. was deducted from the load in bad weather.

Note 14, page 178.—The aeroplane observation squadron with XXI. Corps was under Major M'Crindle, with Story, Norton, and Emmett as Flight Lieutenants. Captain Pownall, and then Lieutenant Mutton, were the artillery liaison officers, who arranged for the planes to go up and the convenient times, and so on. They being gunners, could clear up technical details with the Air Force.

Note 15, page 139.—The Royal Garrison Artillery batteries of the XXI. Corps engaged at the third battle of Gaza, with those officers whose names are recollected, and believed correct.

In the XXI. Corps were—97 Heavy Artillery Group, Lieut.-Colonel Kirkpatrick, Adjutant Capt. Conway, Chaplain Rev. Martin, Medical Officer Captain L. H. Lindley, Capt. O. Thatcher, Sigs. Orderly Ofr. Lt. J. C. Summersell.

---

* With heavy horses?

189* Heavy Battery, 60-pounders, Major G. P. Richardson, Lieutenants C. S. Legget, A. Dewar, G. E. Galbreath, W. Kirk.

195* Heavy Battery, 60-pounders, Major E. S. Phillips, Captains A. W. Turner, F. W. Doggett, Lieutenants D. Williams, B. F. Dobb, L. M. Ashley, R. J. R. G. Wreford.

201 * Siege Battery, two eight-inch and two six-inch howitzers, Major Bingham (?).

205 Siege Battery, four six-inch howitzers, Major W. F. F. Scott, M.C., Capt. Brotherton (?).

300* Siege Battery, two eight-inch and two six-inch howitzers, Major W. Hedley, Capt. P. Thompson, Lts. H. Roughton, R. G. Halton, R. L. Dennis, H. D. Jones.

380 Siege Battery, four six-inch howitzers, Major Powell, Capt. Benton, Capt. H. A. Forrest, Lts. F. D. C. Sumner, Laugharne, C. R. Leach, T. G. Nowell.

Also 100 Heavy Artillery Group, Lt.-Col. W. H. Moore, adjutant, Capt. B. A. Farrow, orderly officer, Lt. A. W. Kingdom, medical officer, Capt. E. A. P. Brock, and Capt. Ludlow, Signals Lt. Pinsent.

10 Heavy Battery, 60-pounders, Capts. A. R. Newlands, T. W. Gilbert, Lts. C. O. B. Dickenson, H. R. Sallowes, B. J. Gibson.

43 Siege Battery, two 6-inch Mark VII. guns, Major A. Thompson, Capt. Greenwell Lax (killed in Macedonia), Capt. H. A. Shaw, Lt. Woodall, Jones, H. G. Taylor, A. Wilson, F. E. Vincent.

134 Siege Battery, four six-inch howitzers, Major H. G. Bagnall, Capt. M. Burns, L. Fielden (?), Lts. W. W. Kerr, J. C. Irving, V. L. S. Bethell, H. G. T. de Sausmarez, F. Anns.

379 Siege Battery, four six-inch howitzers, Major G. Oates, Capt. J. P. Sargent, Lts. C. W. S. Hay, H. P. H. Williams, J. Pickerell, L. Crosland.

422 Siege Battery, four six-inch howitzers, Major
W. Boyd, Capt. W. A. Hine, Lts. C. D. Grimwade,
S. Farley, Mainwaring, Ehrman, Langley.

423 Siege Battery, four eight-inch howitzers, Major
C. M. Grant Govan, Capt. E. P. Johnston, Lts. H. W.
George, H. F. Hearne.

Also 102 Heavy Artillery Group, Lt.-Col. P. N. G.
Reade, adjutant, Capt. C. F. E. Patterson, orderly
officer, Lt. J. W. King, medical officer, Capt. B. A.
Norman.

202 Heavy Battery, 60-pounders, Major Charlton
Thompson, Lts. T. L. Evans, F. F. B. Saxsmith, G. S.
Madden, R. V. Hunter.

209 Siege Battery, six-inch howitzers, Major
Tomlinson, Lt. R. L. Bancroft, E. S. Browne, R. V.
Grimston, H. M. M. Robins, Capt. Haskew, afterwards
Staff Captain 21st Corps Heavy Artillery, Rev. A.
Payne.

292 Siege Battery, with two six-inch howitzers
only, Major C. Mucklow, Lt. J. W. Brown.

420 Siege Battery, four six-inch howitzers, Major
H. W. L. Doane, Lts. G. A. Adam, F. Kidsley, T. R.
Adamson, later Capt. C. J. Ellison.

421 Siege Battery, four six-inch howitzers, Major
W. R. Gill (?), Capt. J. M. Carrie, Lts. T. N. D. Burns,
E. M. Gare, J. Cade, S. M. Capper.

424 Siege Battery, four eight-inch howitzers, Major
W. C. Holden, Lts. T. H. Formby, H. H. Naylor, T. W.
Hunter, later Capt. I. R. Cox.

Batteries underlined left the Egyptian Expeditionary Force in the early months of 1918. Those
marked * are from a list of Sept. 1918.

Later than this record 100 Group transferred two
Mk. VII. guns, 43 S.B., and four 6-inch howitzers, probably 422 S.B., to 97 Group; and 102 Group transferred

six 6-inch howitzers, probably 421 S.B., and the available half* of 292 S.B. to 97 Group, either temporarily for bombardment or permanently. Later on there joined 100 Heavy Artillery Group, Dec. 1917.

15 Heavy Battery, 60-pounders, Major M'Cartny, Capt. A. H. Bunning, Lts. W. G. P. Stirling, A. D. Peacock, F. L. Houlton, E. Lyford, C. A. Gray.

181 Heavy Battery, 60-pounders, Major P. W. Justice, Capt. A. J. Holt, Lts. Atkinson, H. Gandy, D. P. Cousin, C. J. Hipkins, R. A. F. M. Saunders, D. Mason.

Justice went as Brigade Major to Heavy Artillery 20th Corps and Peacocke succeeded; and the XXI. Corps Heavy Artillery was as shown on page 162.

The writer is sorry this list is incomplete but hopes that any one with a further record of names will let him see it.

Note 16, page 162.—The staff of the 21st Corps Heavy Artillery were Brigade Major H. G. Bagnall, Counter-battery Capt. Armitage, Lt. R. L. Bancroft, Staff-Lieut. Intelligence J. C. Brookhouse, Staff Capt. R. S. Haskew, Signals Capt. Parks (Parkes?), Mechanical Transport Army Service Corps Major Sanders, Capt. G. R. Morriss.

Note 17, page 163.—The 95th Heavy Artillery group (Lt.-Col. A. H. Moberly, D.S.O.) came from Italy with the following batteries in his group. The names of officers appear to be the same as shown for the 19th Sept. 1918, note 18, with the following exceptions:— 334 Siege battery, Lts. Tomkins, G. Good; 304 Siege battery, Major Campbell, Lts. O. J. Porter, A. Eggar; 314 Siege battery, Major R. M. Powell, Lt. A. Ryrie; 320 Siege battery, Major K. F. Dunsterville (Dunstable?), Capt. W. R. Brazier, Lts. W. R. O. Melville, A. S. Williams, C. H. Calder, C. J. Cutting, A. D.

* Half believed lost at sea.

Crombie; 322 Siege battery, Major T. S. Couper, Capt. H. G. Merrick, Lts. A. J. H. Lea, F. G. Soper, M. Stoner, A. Pender. Major J. P. Scott, joined 5th Feb. 1918. 394 Siege battery, Lt. A. T. Williams. Also 392 Siege Battery, Major Percival, and went to Mesopotamia; 320 and 322 to Salonika in May.

Note 18, page 189.—The 95th Heavy Artillery Brigade for the battle of 19th September, 1918, consisted of—Headquarters, Lt.-Col. A. H. Moberly. D.S.O.; Adjutant, Capt. E. Webster; Orderly Officer, Lt. H. Gandy; Chaplain (R.C.), Father Ward; Medical Officer, Capt. J. Appleyard; Signals, Bell; A.S.C. Mechanical Transport, Lumsden.

304 Siege Battery, Major T. S. Couper, Capt. J. H. M. O'Farrell, Lts. C. C. Alexander, J. C. S. B. Cooke, T. A. Walker, O. J. Peskett, C. C. R. Worster, P. Williams, and later W. Deptford.

314 Siege Battery, Major G. T. Ford, Capt. I. Benton, Lts. W. Thorpe, C. H. Akehurst, W. H. Worth, L. Fielden, W. H. Grover, H. J. W. Blayney, and later, in October, J. H. Malcolmson, A. J. Hayes, J. E. Mitchell, P. G. Richens.

181 Heavy Battery, Major C. L. Peacocke, Major T. M. Brotherton (?), Capt. A. J. Hoult (? Holt), Lts. D. B. Cousin, C. J. Hipkins, L. Atkinson, D. Mason, J. Sanderson, C. C. Hawkes, C. H. Ray.

394 Siege Battery, Major H. C. E. Routh, Capt. E. C. Burges, Lts. H. C. G. Ellis, A. M. Murray, J. R. Peters, W. Tupper; two 5.9-inch captured guns, Lt. W. Thorpe. 394 from Mesopotamia June 1918.

Note 19, page 189.—The 100th Heavy Artillery Brigade for the battle of 19th September, 1918, consisted of—Headquarters, Lt.-Col. E. D. Matthews; Adjutant, Capt. B. A. Farrow; Orderly Officer, Lt. A. W. Kingdon; Medical Officer, Captain Ludlow.

134 Siege Battery, Major M'Cartney, Capt. M. Burns, Lts. J. C. Irving, F. Anns, W. J. Salter, W. W. Kerr, A. D. Swift, S. G. Brown.

43 Siege Battery, Capt. W. A. V. Thomas, Lts. F. E. Vincent, H. G. Taylor, J. B. Walton.

300 Siege Battery, Major W. Hedley, Capt. P. Thompson, Lts. H. Roughton, H. D. Jones, J. C. Hatton. W. F. Dillow, R. L. Dennis.

15 Heavy Battery, Major H. A. G. Chamier, Capts. C. D. O. Pugh, A. H. Bunning, Lts. W. G. P. Stirling, A. D. Peacock, F. L. Houghton, E. Lyford, C. A. Gray.

Three 4.7 inch guns from coast defence, Maj. S. B. Jones.

On 14th September, 1918, Lt.-Col. W. H. Moore, D.S.O., had been obliged to relinquish through illness, after over a year's command of the group and brigade in Palestine.

Note 20, page 189.—The 102nd Heavy Artillery Brigade for the battle of 19th September, 1918, consisted of—Headquarters, Lt.-Col. F. P. Hutchinson, D.S.O.; Adjutant, Capt. T. L. Evans; Orderly Officer, Lt. J. W. King; Medical Officer, Capt. B. A. Norman; Transport Capt. H. Borton.

209 Siege Battery, Major S. C. Tomlinson; Capt. H. C. Tomkins, Lts. H. M. M. Robbins, G. B. Shiel, R. V. Grimston.

380 Siege Battery, Major R. E. Apletre, Capt. H. A. Forrest, Lts. F. D. C. Sumner, C. R. Leach, T. G. Nowell.

189 Heavy Battery, Major G. P. Richardson, Lts. C. S. Leggat, A. Dewar, G. E. Galbreath, W. Kirk.

202 Heavy Battery, Major P. Doig, D.S.O.; Capt. T. W. Gilbert, Lts. T. Dymcock, G. S. Madden.

Note 21, pages 187, 189.—The 96th Heavy Artillery Brigade, which came from the 20th Corps to reinforce the 21st Corps, consisted of—Headquarters, Lt.-Col. W. C. P. Russell, D.S.O.; Adjutant, Capt. J. E. Braham; Orderly Officer, Lt. H. White; Medical Officer, Capt. V. C. James, Sigs. Lt. F. R. Smith, Rev. H. Handford, M.A.

378 Siege Battery, Major D. B. C. Sladen, Capt. Gossip, Lts. L. G. Steers, H. W. Claxton, G. Reader, W. R. Armstrong, F. E. Stanford, J. T. Wellbelove.

383 Siege Battery, Capt. G. M. Carrie, Capt. E. G. Henry, Lts. J. E. Whitehead, F. H. Baker, J. C. Buckley, R. S. Andrews.

440 Siege Battery, Major C. A. E. Miller, Capt. H. N. Sowdon, Lts. J. V. Campbell, W. Rhodes, R. R. Norman, H. Williams, W. R. D. Fairbairn.

91 Heavy Battery, Major R. H. Clarkson, Capt. A. A. Cummings, Lts. R. J. L. Penfold, A. Boyd, A. Hewitt, J. D. Fell, W. E. B. Dove, L. F. Green.

Attached: 422 Siege Battery, Major H. A. Shaw, Capt. J. C. Brookhouse, Lts. C. L. Mainwaring, S. Farley, J. C. Summersell, E. L. Thorold, V. L. Bethell, Ehrman, Langley.

334 Siege Battery, Major A. H. M. Cherry, Capt. F. J. Somerscales, Lts. E. C. Smith, C. W. Graham, S. M. Capper, W. E. Jones.

Four more 6-inch howitzers, of which the identity has not been traced.

422 and 334 Siege Batteries came from 97 Heavy Artillery Brigade—Lt.-Col. O. K. Tancock; Adjutant, Capt. R. Acton; Orderly Officer, Lt. E. M. Gare; Medical Officer, Capt. J. Cook, Rev. O. G. O. Larr, M.A.

Capt. M. D. Dawe, of 421, commanded a captured 5.9-inch enemy howitzer battery on the 20th Corps front. called "Fritz Battery."

Note 22, pages 130/1.—13 Heavy Battery in Macedonia in 1916 to 1917 had Major F. W. Vander Kiste, Capt. A. E. Jordan, Lts. R. S. Haskew, Groves, R. J. Audrey, Boyce, R. S. Moxon.

If any names of officers of the formations mentioned (pages 130/1) are sent to the writer he will record them. They may include attached medical, signalling, Army Service Corps officers, and officers of the Chaplains Department; also balloon and Flying Corps officers working with the R.G.A. mentioned.

Note 23, page 93.—No. 27 (Major O. K. Tancock) and No. 28 (Major C. E. Forestier-Walker) Mountain Batteries mobilised, No. 27 on 14th August. On 10th September it joined force "C," and left Abbottabad on 13th, embarked in the s.s. *Bandra,* and sailed in a convoy of about 33 ships, most of which went north from Bombay with the Indian divisions for Europe to France. Five or six ships went to British East Africa to Killindini on 3rd October, 1914. 27 went by rail at once to Nairobi. They fought, using the shield designed by O. K. Tancock and Capt. A. J. Farfan, on 4th November, 1914, at close range to the Germans. 28 Mountain Battery fought at Tanga, German East Africa, about 3rd or 4th November, 1914, firing their guns from on board ship; they did not land. Both batteries stayed fighting in German East Africa, at any rate, till end of 1916.

Note 24, page 141.—At 11 p.m. Thursday, 1st November, 1917, the real attack on Gaza by the British infantry started with an advance on a strong Turkish outwork (near Red House, see map) called Umbrella Hill, which was taken. It was said this led to the 52nd Division adopting an umbrella as their mark. The enemy opened an intense fire on the British lines. For instance. at one time five 5.9-inch batteries were

reported to be firing on Sampson's Ridge in the heavy
sand hills west of Red House. At 11 p.m. all counter-
battery guns, including the 100th Heavy Artillery
Group, opened fire for neutralising the enemy's guns
in this neighbourhood. A definite neutralisation pro-
gramme had been previously drawn up: generally
speaking, for a gun to neutralise each suspected
position of the enemy's guns which were able to fire on
the attack.

At first the 100th Heavy Artillery Group's fire did
not seem to interfere seriously with the fire of the
enemy's guns. A report, however, came in from
Captain Bate of the Royal Flying Corps. He had
remained flying over the enemy's lines after dark on
that evening. This report gave information of fresh
enemy batteries as active, and he gave their positions
on the map. By 11.45 p.m. the 100th Group had turned
fire from their guns on to these fresh positions. This
new fire produced the desired effect of disconcerting the
intense fire of the enemy on the British infantry. For
the rest of that night the 100th Heavy Artillery Group
appeared to keep the enemy's gun fire down and well in
hand, and so to diminish the enemy's power to damage
the attacking British infantry.

Note 25, page 171.—At the battle of Mejdel Yaba
the Heavy Artillery put some batteries of the 95th and
102nd Groups into a very exposed position north east
of Mulebbis, whence they were able to fire in reverse
on the Mejdel Yaba salient of the Turkish defences.

Note 26, page 86.—Kitchener gave a party on
Christmas night, 1906, to those of his staff who were
lonely and had no other gaiety to go to. About a
dozen were there, and Kitchener was telling about his
various collections, especially from China. He was
very keen on porcelain. The conversation turned to
jade, and Oswald said he knew a little about jade, as

his battery was in the original expedition to the jade mines. He mentioned that the jade mines in Upper Burma north-west of Mogoung were the only source of the true Chinese sacred jade, that it had a peculiar green tinge. To get it clear from the white jade the heavy blocks of jade stone went—in the days he was speaking of—on men's backs for many marches, and ultimately reached Mandalay. In Mandalay the green stone was carefully cut out of the white, by means of polishing wheels coated with ruby dust, until only the green stone was left. Ruby dust was used on account of the hardness of the jade stone. The shapes which the green stones took, when cleared of the white stone, were accustomed in 1888 to determine their price. It was said a small green jade cup cost Lord William Beresford two thousand rupees (say £130). After dinner Kitchener was showing some rarities, among others a Mandarin's staff of sorts in white jade. Oswald was surprised to see that a material as common as white jade should be made into such things, but did not say anything. Later Kitchener said, " I want to show the jade man something." Oswald went over, and saw a beautiful porcelain jar with a cover. He thought it was funny to show him porcelain, as he knew nothing about it. The Chief was looking at him, and then Oswald saw inset on the knob on the top of the jar a piece of jade of the best green jade. " Oh, yes," he said, " that is beautiful jade," and Kitchener smiled broadly. It seemed so characteristic of Kitchener, who no doubt had always to guard himself and to discriminate between those who knew and those who said they knew.

INDEX.